신경향

종합 **영작문** 클리닉

신규철(申奎澈) K. C. Shin, Ph. D.
고려대학교 영어교육과 졸업(학사)
한국외국어대학교 대학원 영어과 졸업(석사)
고려대학교 대학원 영어영문학과 졸업(박사, 영어교육학 전공)
미국 하와이대학교(University of Hawaii at Manoa) 언어학과 연구교수
고려대학교, 한국외국어대학교, 서울시립대학교, 동덕여자대학교 강사
공군장교 복무(교육장교)
Pearson Education Korea(롱맨) 컨설턴트

범태평양 응용언어학회(Pan-Pacific Association of Applied Linguistics) 이사
현대영어교육학회 이사, 한국영어어문교육학회 이사, 한국영어학회 이사
한국영어독서교육학회 회장
극동대학교 영어학과 교수(언어교육연구소 소장)

●●● 저서
영어습득론 입문, 연구방법론의 이해, 영어교육학, 현대영어교육이론과 적용,
신경향 핵심영문독해, 90단계 기초영문법, 60단계 핵심영문법, Power Vocabulary in Reading,
English Idioms 800, 한국인을 위한 자동화 영어학습법,
자발적 다독법을 통한 통합적 읽기교육 연구 외 다수

신경향 종합**영작문** 클리닉

2쇄 • 2012년 9월 27일
저자 • 신규철 / 발행인 • 이성모 / 발행처 • 도서출판 동인
주소 • 서울시 종로구 명륜동 2가 237 아남주상복합Ⓐ 118호 / 등록 • 제1-1599호
TEL • (02) 765-7145 / FAX • (02) 765-7165
E-mail • dongin60@chollian.net / Homepage • donginbook.co.kr

ISBN 978-89-5506-362-2 13740   정가 12,000원

신경향

종합 **영작문** 클리닉

신규철 지음

도서출판 **동인**

PREFACE

현대사회를 살아가는 우리에게 세계어로서의 영어는 이제 우리 생활의 한 부분이 되었고, 경쟁사회를 헤치고 나아가는 우리에게, 영어는 필수 자산이 된 지도 오래 되었다. 이런 상황에서 볼 때, 영어 실력 향상을 위해, 영어에 대한 효과적인 지침서를 찾는다는 것은 매우 중요하다고 볼 수 있다.

한편, 우리는 주변에서 영어의 네 기능인 읽기·쓰기·말하기·듣기에 대한 수많은 책을 접하고 있지만, 그 중에서 쓰기 분야에 대한 효과적인 지침서를 찾아보기가 상대적으로 힘들다는 것을 알 수 있다. 이것은 영작문에 대한 효율적인 방법을 찾기가 그 만큼 힘들다는 것을 보여주는 예라고 할 수 있다. 따라서 필자는 학습자들이 짧은 시간에 효과적인 작문 연습을 할 수 있는 교재가 필요하다고 생각하게 되었다.

본서는 학교 현장에서 영작문을 학습하는 학생들의 보다 심화된 영작 실력을 위해 만들어졌다.

1장은 …… 영작문을 하는 학습자들이 흔히 범하기 쉬운 오류들을 분석하여, 틀리기 쉬운 영작문 패턴을 구문적 설명과 함께 해설하였다.

2장은 …… 영작문에 비롯한, 연어(collocation)와 자주 사용되는 필수 패턴을 정리하고 연습을 할 수 있도록 했다.

3장은 …… 에세이 영작을 효과적으로 하기 위해, 주요 영어구문에서 많이 사용되는 표현들을 그대로 써보는 카피 영작문 연습을 할 수 있도록 하였다. 또한 종합적으로 많이 사용되는 영어 표현을 중심으로 수준 있는 글을 써보게 하였다.

4장은 …… 토플 에세이를 비롯한 에세이 영작문의 기법과 요령을 소개하고 연습할 수 있도록 만들었다.

끝으로 이 『신경향 종합영작문 클리닉』이 학교 현장에서 영작문을 공부하는 학습자들에게 조그마한 도움이 될 수 있기를 바라며, 이 책이 나오기까지 많은 격려와 도움을 주신 동인출판사 사장님과 편집진에게 감사의 말씀을 드리는 바이다.

2008년 8월 저자 신규철

TABLE OF CONTENTS

I. 영작문 클리닉

1. 단문 (Simple Sentences) ······ 10
2. 복문 (Compound Sentences) ······ 20
3. 중문 (Complex Sentences) ······ 22
4. 동사와 시제 (Verb & Tense) ······ 25
5. 수동구문과 능동구문 ······ 28
6. 중요 가정법 구문 ······ 30
7. 주의해야 할 단어 ······ 31
8. 상황별 부사의 쓰임 ······ 34
9. 틀리기 쉬운 영작문형 ······ 35
10. 영작문 필수구문 정리 ······ 39

II. 영작문에 꼭 필요한 COLLOCATION

1. 영작문에 꼭 필요한 COLLOCATION ······ 72
2. 주제별 영작 필수 패턴 ······ 136
3. 영작에 필요한 속담 ······ 144

III. 주요 영작문 따라쓰기

1. 주요 구문 따라쓰기 (I) ······ 174
2. 주요 구문 따라쓰기 (II) ······ 189
3. 종합 영작문 연습 ······ 206

IV. 에세이 영작문

1. 훌륭한 에세이 10계명 ······ 212
2. 영작문의 단계 ······ 213
3. 에세이 단락의 구성 ······ 214
4. 토플 에세이 (TWE) ······ 216

영작문 클리닉

신경향 종합영작문 클리닉 PART

I.

1 단문
SIMPLE SENTENCES

1. 주어(Subject)

동사와 함께 기능을 하며 문장의 핵을 이룬다.
〈명사 · 대명사 · 부정사 · 동명사 · 의문사절 · 동격절〉 등이 주어 역할을 한다.

- **Paul** was a fine person. (명사)
- The dirt-covered old **car** suddenly collapsed. (명사)
- **Religion** is a comfort to many people. (명사)
- **To act** promptly can save many lives. (부정사)
- **Seeing** is believing. (동명사)
- **Honesty** is considered a virtue. (명사)
- **It** is a new bookcase. (대명사)
- **What they found** surprised me. (절)
- **Where we go** depend on the job opportunities. (의문사절)
- **Whether it rains or not** doesn't matter. (의문사절)
- **The fact that he survived the accident** is a miracle. (the fact that-절)

작문연습   주어진 주어로 시작하는 문장을 쓰시오.

① 소년들은 소녀들에게 계란을 던졌다. (The boys)

② 비행기가 안전하게 착륙했다. (The plane)

③ 그녀의 성실함은 의심받을 수 있다. (her sincerity)

④ 이 순간에 후퇴한다면 현명할 것이다. (to retreat)

⑤ 이 자리에 지원하는 것은 그에게 어렵다. (applying)

⑥ 민주주의는 정부의 이상적 형태이다. (democracy)

영·작·특·강 ― 주어의 개념

주부의 중심이 되는 말. 〈～은, ～는, ～이, ～가〉로 해석.
명사·대명사, 그 상당어구 (명사구·명사절)가 주어가 될 수 있다.
단독으로 주부를 이루기보다는 수식어와 같이 주부를 이루는 경우가 많다.

- **My friend, Jim** went to Austria to study music. (명사·명사구)
- **They** play tennis every weekend. (대명사)
- **To learn a foreign language** is very difficult. (명사구·부정사구)
- **Swimming in the river in this weather** is very dangerous. (명사구·동명사구)
- **That he is honest** is known to everybody in the village. (명사절·that절)
- **The true** is beautiful. (the + 형용사 = 추상명사)
- **What I did for him yesterday** hurts his feelings. (관계대명사절)

모범답안

① The boys threw eggs at the girls.
② The plane landed safely.
③ Her sincerity can be questioned.
④ To retreat at this moment would be wise.
⑤ Applying for this position is difficult.
⑥ Democracy is the ideal form of government

2. 동사(Verb)

주어와 함께 작용하여 문장의 핵심적인 의미를 준다.
동사는 주어와 결합하여 수와 인칭, 그리고 단수-복수의 일치를 지킨다.

- The scientist will **be** in Hawaii soon. (존재동사)
- The soldiers **slept** for 10 hours. (행위동사)
- Everyone **appears** to be energetic. (감정·감각동사)
- This banana **tastes** good. (감정·감각동사)

작문연습   주어진 동사를 사용하여 문장을 쓰시오.

① 많은 학생들이 전에 그곳에 있었다. (were)

....

② 그들은 많은 훌륭한 성질을 갖고 있다. (possess)

....

③ 암탉이 자신의 알 위에 앉아 있다. (sat)

....

④ 장미는 향기가 좋다. (smelled)

....

모범답안
① Many students were there before.
② They possess many admirable qualities.
③ The hen sat on its eggs.
④ The rose smelled good.

영·작·특·강 — 동사의 개념

술부의 중심이 되는 말 〈~이다, ~하다〉로 해석.
주어의 동작이나 상태를 나타낸다. 보통 조동사까지 포함하여 일컫는다.
- I **play** tennis every weekend.
- Man **cannot live** without water.

3. 주어-동사의 일치

전치사구 앞에 있는 주어에 동사를 일치시킨다.

- **The men** [on top] [of the red roof] **are** drunk.
- **None** [of the men] **has** signed the contract.
- **The boys** [in the park] **are** fighting.

작문연습 다음 예문을 영작하시오.

① 뉴욕의 동부지역 출신의 학자들이 회의를 열고 있다. (scholars / conference)

....

② 어두운 강의 다른 편에 있는 작은 집의 아이들이 우리에게 손을 흔들고 있다. (wave at)

....

③ 저 위험한 범죄자들 중의 한 사람이 그의 형이다. (criminals)

....

모범답안
① Scholars from the eastern part of New York are holding a conference.
② The children in the small house on the other side of the dark river wave at us.
③ One of those dangerous criminals is his brother.

I. 영작문 클리닉

4. 목적어(Object)

동사가 나타내는 동작이나 상태의 대상이다.

- He always invite **Tom** to the party.
- They opened **the door**.
- She likes **football**.

작문연습 다음 주어진 말을 이용하여 문장을 영작하시오.

① Jane은 그를 아주 많이 좋아한다. (love / so much)

....

② 그는 휴대폰을 갖고 있다. (cell phone)

....

③ 경찰들은 그녀를 뒤쫓고 있다. (run after)

....

④ 나는 새 시계를 좋아한다. (new watch)

....

모범답안
① Jane loves him so much.　　② He has a cell phone.
③ The police run after her.　　④ I like the new watch.

5. 보어(Complement)

동사만으로는 글이 불완전할 때 〈주어·목적어〉의 성질·상태를 보충 설명하는 말로, 〈명사·대명사·형용사 및 그 상당어구〉가 보어가 된다. 주격 보어는 주어의 성질·상태를 보충 설명하며, 목적격 보어는 목적어의 성질·상태를 보충 설명한다.

- He looks **happy**. (형용사)
- He sat **reading** the newspaper. (현재분사)
- He is **a famous Korean artist** in the world. (명사)
- My hobby is **collecting** stamps. (동명사)
- I had my watch **stolen**. (과거분사)
- I had my brother **repair** my bike. (동사원형)
- I saw her **enter** the room. (동사원형)
- I kept them **waiting** at the gate for an hour. (현재분사)

작문연습

다음 주어진 말을 이용하여 영작하시오.

① Alex는 영화배우이다. (movie star)

② 그의 선생님은 유명하다. (famous)

③ Sarah는 행복해 보인다. (happy)

④ 나의 스웨터가 나를 따뜻하게 해준다. (keep / warm)

⑤ 그녀는 그가 거리를 건너는 것을 보았다. (cross / street)

모범답안

① Alex is a movie star.
② His teacher is famous.
③ Sarah looks happy.
④ My sweater keeps me warm.
⑤ She watches him cross the street.

6. 절(Clause)

〈주어 + 동사〉의 형태로 문장의 일부를 이루는 것을 절이라 하며, 문법적 구조에 따라 〈등위절 · 주절 · 종속절〉로 나뉜다.

1. 등위절

등위접속사 〈and · but · for · or · so〉 등이 각 문장을 대등하게 연결해 준다.

• He is a scholar **and** his wife is a teacher.

작문연습

주어진 말을 이용하여 영작하시오.

① 그녀는 아들 하나가 있으며, 그녀의 아들은 수학을 가르친다. (teach / mathematics)

2. 주절

두 개 이상의 절로 이루어진 문장 가운데 글의 주체가 되는 주된 절을 말하며, 종속절을 제외한 나머지 부분이다.

• **I will let her know this fact** when she comes back.
• **He studies hard** that he may succeed.

작문연습

주어진 말을 이용하여 영작하시오.

② 나는 그가 곧 회복할 것이라고 믿는다. (believe / recover / soon)

모범답안

① She has a son and her son teaches mathematics.
② I believe that he will recover soon.

3. 종속절

종속절은 주절에 종속된 절로서 문장 내의 역할에 따라 〈명사절·형용사절·부사절〉로 나누어진다.

(1) 명사절 : 명사처럼 〈주어·목적어·보어〉의 역할을 한다.
- **What he did for us in that situation** is absolutely right. (주어)
  (그가 우리를 위해 그 상황에서 했던 것은 절대적으로 옳다.)
- He said **that his girl friend had left him forever**. (목적어)
  (그는 그의 여자 친구가 그를 영원히 떠났다고 말했다.)
- This is **what I eagerly want**. (보어)
  (이것은 내가 몹시 원했던 것이다.)

작문연습

주어진 말을 이용하여 영작하시오.

③ 그들이 하고 있는 것은 정부의 지지를 받고 있다. (what / support / government)

．．．

(2) 형용사절 : 앞의 명사(선행사)를 수식하는 절로, 연결어에는 다음과 같은 종류가 있다.

① 관계대명사절 : who·which·that 등.
- The boy **who is playing the piano** is my brother.
  (피아노를 치고 있는 그 소년은 나의 형이다.)
- This is the gift **which I bought for my mother**.
  (이것은 내가 나의 어머니를 위해 샀던 선물이다.)

작문연습

주어진 말을 이용하여 영작하시오.

④ 내가 해야 하는 모든 것은 경기에서 최선을 다하는 것이다.
   (all / have to / best / game)

．．．

모범답안

③ What they are doing is supported by the government.
④ All that I have to do was just to try my best in the game.

2 **관계부사절** : when · where · why · how 등
- I remember the day **when Korean War broke out**.
  (나는 한국전쟁이 일어났던 날을 기억한다.)
- This is the village **where I was brought up in my childhood**.
  (이곳은 내가 어린 시절에 자랐던 마을이다.)

작문연습 주어진 말을 이용하여 영작하시오.

⑤ 나는 그가 한 마디 말도 없이 그 나라를 떠났던 이유를 모른다.
(why / leave / without saying a word)

⑥ 나에게 네가 이 복잡한 퍼즐을 어떻게 풀었는지 말해라.
(how / solve / complicate / puzzle)

(3) 부사절 : 주절의 앞 또는 뒤에서 동사·형용사·부사를 수식하며, 〈시간·원인·장소·이유·목적·결과·조건·양보〉 등의 여러 가지 뜻을 나타낸다.

> 연결 접속사로는 as, when, while, after, before, as soon as, till, until, because, since, if, unless, though, although, even though 등이 있다.

- He died **when he was 95**. (시간)
  (그는 나이가 95살 되었을 때 죽었다.)
- **If it is fine tomorrow**, we will play soccer in the ground. (조건)
  (만약 내일 날씨가 좋다면, 우리는 운동장에서 축구를 할 것이다.)

모범답안
⑤ I don't know the reason why he left the country without saying a word.
⑥ Tell me how you solve this complicate puzzle.

작문연습 다음 주어진 말을 이용하여 영작하시오.

⑦ 그는 경찰을 보자마자 도망갔다. (as soon as / police / run away)

....

⑧ 그가 돌아 올 때까지 기다리자. (wait / until / come back)

....

영·작·특·강 — 연결어의 종류

1 접속사 : that (~을), whether / if (~인지 아닌지) 등

- I wonder **if** he will come here or not.
- I don't know **whether** she will receive the prize.
- I think **that** he is very sincere and industrious.

2 의문사 : who, what, how, when, where, why 등

- **What** do you think he did last night?
- I want to know **how** to ride a bike.

3 관계사 : who (선행사가 사람일 때 연결)
which that (선행사가 사물일 때 연결)
what (선행사 개념이 포함된 관계사 : ~하는 것)

- The policeman **who** reported the accident has red hair.
- I have a TV **which (that)** is made in Korea.
- **What** he said is not always true.

모범답안
⑦ As soon as he saw the police, he ran away.
⑧ Let's wait until he comes back.

2 복문
COMPOUND SENTENCES

1. 등위접속사

⟨and · but · or · for · yet · so⟩를 접속사로 사용하여 대등하게 문장을 연결하여 준다.

- The president arrived early, **yet** he missed the prime minister.
- Jane went to the beach, **but** she did not find her friend.

영·작·특·강 — 접속부사의 역할

접속부사는 문장의 인과관계를 나타내주는 중요한 역할을 한다.

- ~의 결과로서 : accordingly; consequently; hence; thus; therefore; then
- ~에도 불구하고 : nevertheless; however
- 게다가 : moreover; furthermore; in addition

2. 상관접속사

⟨either A or B⟩ ⟨neither A nor B⟩ ⟨not only A but also B⟩를 이용하여 쓰는 구문으로 문장을 서로 상관지워 나타낸다.

- **Either** John will go to Mary **or** Mary will come to John.
- **Neither** did the enemy appear **nor** did the fog lift.
- **Not only** did the delegation reach Iraq quickly, **but** they **also** brought good news with them.

3. 세미콜론(;) 접속부사 패턴

새로운 문장을 시작시키며, 여러 가지 위치에 나타난다.

> 예) ; accordingly ; however ; then ; consequently ; moreover ; therefore
> ; furthermore ; nevertheless ; otherwise ; hence ; thus

- The strike was called during the harvest; **consequently** much food was spoiled.
- They were invited by the president himself; **nevertheless**, they decided not to go to the party.

작문연습
- 그녀는 John과 필사적으로 결혼하고 싶었다. 그러나 Peter가 돈이 더 많았다.

4. 기타 세미콜론의 의미

세미콜론은 마침표나 and의 뜻을 갖는다. 상호 관련된 주절 사이에서 and의 의미를 대신한다.

- Herry went to England; Mary followed shortly
- We do not seek power; we do not seek glory.

작문연습
- 훈련생들이 파업을 일으켰다. 그래서 모든 철도 운송이 지연되었다.

모범답안
- She wanted to marry John desperately; however, Peter had more money.
- The trainmen went on strike; all rail shipment was delayed.

3 중문
COMPLEX SENTENCES

중문은 주절과 1개 이상의 종속절로 구성된 문장을 말한다.

1. 주절 + 종속절

- The men fished **while** the women plowed the fields.
- She has a long known the man **who** is in love with you.

2. 종속절 + 주절

- **When** John arrived, he was greeted with kisses.
- **Whatever** happens, I still love you

3. 주절 속에 종속절이 포함된 문장

- My friend Paul, **whom you do not know**, is madly in love.
- The company **that hired you** is going bankrupt.

4. 종속절이 문장의 주어, 목적어 등의 단위로 쓰일 때

- **That you do not love** me hurts my pride.
- I am thinking about **what this poem means**.
- She thanked **whoever had sent the money**.

작문연습

① 그 도둑은 경찰이 떠날 때까지 숨어 있었다.

② 그녀가 누구이든 간에 나는 그녀와 함께 나가지 않을 것이다.

③ 우리가 믿었던 그녀가 사라졌다.

④ 그는 그의 아버지가 한 것을 신봉하고 있다.

영·작·특·강 — 콜론·세미콜론·콤마·대시의 차이

1. 콜론(:)

(1) 기대와 열거, 인용 등을 알릴 때 쓴다. 〈다음과 같은〉의 의미를 지닌다.
   Pay attention to these directions:
   Light the fuses carefully.
   Run rapidly!

(2) 긴 인용문을 도입할 때 쓰인다.
   In the Dhammapada, a book of Buddhist sayings, one will find this quotation: "A man should first direct himself in the way he should go. Only then should he instruct others; a wise man will do so and not grow weary."

(3) 비즈니스 편지의 인사말 다음에 사용된다.
   • Dear Sirs:
   • Gentlemen:
   • Dear Ms. Gardner:

2. 세미콜론(;)

(1) 복문에서 어떤 등위접속어 앞에서 사용된다.
   예) ; accordingly ; however ; then ; consequently ; moreover
       ; therefore ; furthermore ; nevertheless ; otherwise ; hence
       ; thus

모범답안

① The thief hid until the policeman left.
② Whoever she is, I will not go out with her.
③ The woman whom we trusted has disappeared.
④ He believes in what his father did.

(2) 마침표(.) 대신 2개의 주절 사이에서 쓸 수 있다.
(3) 일련의 복잡한 단어, 구, 절에서 분명하게 다루기 위해 콤마(,) 대신 쓰인다.
예) Members of the band included John, clarinetist; Mary, tuba player; Alex, drummer; and Smith, trumpeter.

3. 콤마(,)

(1) 단어, 구, 절 형용사가 나열될 때 쓰인다.
(2) 종속절과 주절 사이에 쓰인다.
- Before he arrived in the U.S., Professor Shin learned English thoroughly.
- After many years of travel in Amazon jungles, Keren returned home.

(3) 연결부사가 문장의 가운데 올 때 양쪽에 콤마로 연결한다.
- He, on the other hand, decided to go.
- They did not, as a matter of fact, come near here.

(4) 비제한적 용법의 동격이나 관계절에서 콤마를 쓴다.
- Jane, his friend, lives in Hawaii.
  cf) His friend Jane lives in Hawaii. (제한적)
- He gave the money to Wada, who is my father-in-law.
  cf) It was a report which he desperately needed. (제한적)

(5) 의미를 분명하게 구별하기 위해서 쓴다.
- When the plane flies over, the children will cheer.
  cf) When the plane flies over the children will cheer
- However, they tried hard to win.
- However hard they tried, they could not win.

(6) 날짜(March15, 2008), 편지(Sincerely yours) 등에서 쓰인다.

4. 대시(dash; -)

(1) 콤마로 연결되어 있는 말들을 분류하여 문장 중간에 놓게 할 때 사용된다.
- Some of the city's service departments-water, heat, sanitation, and safety-are vitally in need of funds.
- The men in question- Kane, Peterson, and Andrew- deserve awards.

(2) 강조할 때 쓰인다.
- Thousands of young men were killed and injured in Korean War-the longest war in modern history.

(3) 문장 중간에서 괄호 역할을 한다.
- His idea-one which just suddenly popped into his head-seems like a very sound approach.
- The automobile-he had always dreamed of owning a fleet of them-lay in ruins at the bottom of the cliff.

4. 동사와 시제
VERB & TENSE

1. 현재시제

현재 : Ton **build** the house.
현재완료 : Tom **has built** the house.
현재진행 : Tom **is building** the house.
현재완료진행 : Tom **has been building** the house.

2. 과거시제

과거 : Tom **built** the house.
과거완료 : Tom **had built** the house.
과거진행 : Tom **was building** the house.
과거완료진행 : Tom **had been building** the house.

3. 미래시제

미래 : Tom **will build** the house.
미래완료 : Tom **will have built** the house.
미래진행 : Tom **will be building** the house.
미래완료진행 : Tom **will have been building** the house.

작문연습 다음 문장을 주어진 시제에 맞게 쓰시오.

① (현재) 그녀는 아름답게 그림을 그린다.

....

② (현재완료) 우리들은 서로 오랫동안 사랑해 왔다.

....

③ (현재진행) 그는 조심스럽게 운전 중이다.

....

④ (현재완료진행) 많은 여행객들이 몇 년 동안 이곳을 방문해 오고 있다.

....

⑤ (과거) 그들이 그에게 메달을 수여했다.

....

⑥ (과거완료) 그들은 이미 우리가 그곳에 도착하기 전에 저녁을 주문했다.

....

⑦ (과거진행) 우리는 빵을 잘게 썰고 있었다.

....

⑧ (과거완료진행) 우리는 하루 종일 여행해 왔었지만, 늦게 도착했다.

....

⑨ (미래) 교사들은 보다 적은 수업을 요구할 것이다.

....

⑩ (미래완료) 그들은 내일 오후가 되면 20시간 공부하는 셈이다.

⑪ (미래진행) 상원은 하원이 다른 법안을 토론하는 동안 하나의 법안을 토론하는 중일 것이다.

⑫ (미래완료진행) 그 평의회는 오후 5시가 되면 2주 내내 토론을 하고 있는 중일 것이다.

모범답안

① She paints beautifully.
② We have loved each other for a long time.
③ He is driving carefully.
④ Many tourists have been visiting here for years.
⑤ They presented him with the medal.
⑥ They had already ordered dinner before we arrived there.
⑦ We were slicing the bread.
⑧ We had been traveling all day but had arrived late.
⑨ The teachers will demand smaller classes.
⑩ They will have studied for twenty hours by tomorrow.
⑪ The Senate will be discussing one bill while the House will be debating a different one.
⑫ The council will have been debating for two whole weeks by 5:00 pm

5. 수동구문과 능동구문

- Mr. Jones requests you to deliver this box. (능동구문)
    ▶ You are requested by Mr. Jones to deliver this box. (수동구문)

- Several witnesses saw me. (능동구문)
    ▶ I was seen by several witnesses. (수동구문)

- The king will greet you. (능동구문)
    ▶ You will be greeted by the king. (수동구문)

- The police have detained you. (능동구문)
    ▶ You have been detained by the police. (수동구문)

작문연습

주어진 단어로 시작하여 문장을 완성하시오.

① The new law denies him his rights.

▶ He

② Many people will follow me.

▶ I

③ The president invited them to the Anniversary Ball.

▶ They

④ His girl friend was seen by a psychiatrist.

▶ A psychiatrist

⑤ 2백 명이 그 회사에 의해 고용되고 있다.

▶ Two hundred people

⑥ 그 음악은 매우 커서 멀리 떨어진 곳에서도 들을 수 있었다.

▶ The music

⑦ 그 방은 현재 청소되고 있다.

▶ The room

⑧ 당신에게는 결정할 많은 시간이 주어질 것이다.

▶ You

⑨ 우리의 개는 차에 치었다.

▶ Our dog

⑩ Cathy는 하루에 14시간 일한다고 한다.

▶ It

▶ Cathy

⑪ Jill은 어제 지붕을 수리했다.

▶ Jill

⑫ 나는 네가 이발을 해야 한다고 생각한다.

▶ I think

모범답안

① is denied his rights by the new law.
② will be followed by many people.
③ were invited to the Anniversary Ball by the president.
④ saw his girl friend.
⑤ are employed by the company.
⑥ was very loud and couldn't be heard from a long way away.
⑦ is being cleaned at the moment.
⑧ will be given plenty of time to decide.
⑨ got run over by a car.
⑩ is said that Cathy works 14 hours a day. / is said to work 14 hours a day.
⑪ had the roof repaired yesterday.
⑫ you should get your hair cut.

6 중요 가정법 구문

1. I wish ~가정법 구문 : ~하면 좋겠는데~

- I wish you **were** here now. (가정법 과거)
- I wish you **had been** here at that time. (가정법 과거완료)

2. If절 가정법 구문

- If I **were** king, you **would** be my queen. (가정법 과거)
- If I **had been** king, you **would have been** my queen. (가정법 과거완료)

3. 요구 · 명령 · 소망 동사 + 가정법 현재 구문

require · demand · ask · order · wish 동사 + (should) 원형 동사

- He **stimulated** that all firearms (should) **be** registered.
- They **asked** that the buildings (should) **be** torn down.
- It is the President's **wish** that Sergeant Tawny (should) **be** given the Medal of Honor.

7 주의해야 할 단어

영작에 있어 혼동하기 쉬운 단어들은 단어의 정의와 함께 예문 속에서 비교하는 것이 큰 도움이 될 때가 많다. 몇 가지 예를 보기로 한다.

- accept 받아들이다(동사)   I **accepted** the money with gratitude.
- except 제외하고(전치사)   Everyone **except** me was invited.

- advice 제안(명사)   If you **advise** him not to go, he will heed your advice.
- advise 충고하다(동사)

- affect 영향을 주다(동사)   His views **affected** my decision.
- effect 영향/결과(명사)   The **effect** of the alcohol was immediate.

- all ready 완전히 준비된   I am **all ready** now.
- already 이미/사전에   The meal had **already** been cooked.

- all together 전체적으로/함께   Try singing **all together**.
- altogether 전적으로   You are **altogether** despicable.

- altar 제단(명사)   They stood before the **altar**.
- alter 변경하다(동사)   The company will **alter** its plan.

- cite 인용하다(동사)   He **cited** long passages from the Bible.
- site 장소/위치(명사)   They found a beautiful **site** for their home.
- sight 모습/시력(명사)   It was a beautiful **sight**.

- council 평의회/모임(명사)   The city **council** passed many bills.
- counsel 충고(명사)   He sought **counsel** from the lawyer.
- counsel 충고하다(동사)   He **counseled** me wisely.

- formally 형식적으로/격식을 차리며 (부사)   They were **formally** presented to the present.

• formerly 예전에(부사)	The convict had **formerly** been with the FBI.
• loose 느슨한(형용사)	They set the dog **loose**.
• lose 잃다(동사)	I hope they don't **lose** the diamond.
• past 지나가버린/끝난 상태의(형용사)	They are **past** president of the club.
• passed 〈지나치다〉의 과거, 과거분사형(동사)	The parade **passed** our house.
• principle 원리(명사)	He stuck by his **principles**.
• principal 주요한(형용사)	You are the **principal** character in this play.
• quite 매우(부사)	She is **quite** small.
• quiet 조용한(형용사)	The birds are **quiet** today.

- adapt 적응하다(동사) to make fit or suitable to requirements / to adjust
- adopt 선택하다(동사) to choose for / to take into one's family as a relation

  Would-be parents **adopt** children sometimes. Children, however, seldom get a chance to choose would-be parents. Somehow they **adapt** to each other.

- aid 돕다(동사)/도움(명사) to assist or help/ assistance, help
- aide 도와주는 사람(명사) one who aids or helps, assistant

  One time a general asked an **aide** to **aid** him. And the **aide** obeyed. he **aided** the general. In appreciation for the **aide's aid**, the general ordered a drink for himself and his assistant.

- avert 방향을 돌리다/막다(동사) to turn away or aside from. prevent
- avoid 회피하다(동사) to keep away from, shun, evade

  Mary has a problem in double vision. She knows she ought to **avert** her eyes even though, at long last, a man has made a pass at her. She knows she had better not **avoid** his eyes, or romance once again will have passed her by.

- bazaar 물건을 파는 곳(명사) a place for the sale of goods
- bizarre 괴팍한(형용사) odd, extravagant, or eccentric in style or mode

  "Come with me to the **bazaar**," Peter said. "But remember. Lay off all that **bizarre** stuff!"

- complement 보충하다(동사)　　　something that completes
- compliment 칭찬(명사)　　　　　flattery

　　This jewelry will **complement** your dress.
　　Mary enjoyed the **compliment** paid to her.

- continual 지속적인(간헐적으로)/형용사　a close recurrence in time, in rapid succession
- continuous 지속적인(계속적인)/형용사　without interruption

　　The **continual** ringing of the doorbell bothers me.
　　The ticking of the watch was **continuous**.

- convince 확신하다(동사)　　　to overcome the doubts of
- persuade 설득하다(동사)　　　influencing a person to an action or belief

　　I am **convinced** that you are right and you have **persuaded** me to help you.

- desert 사막(명사)　　　　　　an arid barren land
　　　　버리다, 도망가다(동사)
- dessert 디저트(명사)　　　　　dish served at the end of the end

　　Norman Nomad was not about to **desert** his **dessert** in the **desert**.

- envelop 덮다(동사)　　　　　to cover, to wrap
- envelope 커버(명사)　　　　　a covering

　　Fire will soon **envelop** the entire block.
　　Put a stamp on this **envelope**.

- human 사람(명사)　　　　　　a person
- humane 부드러운, 자상한(형용사)　tender, merciful, considerate

　　His treatment of the prisoners was **humane**.

- may be (두 개의 단어/가능성 표시)　two words to express a possibility
- maybe 아마도(부사)　　　　　perhaps

　　It **may be** going to snow today.
　　Maybe you will finish your task early today.

I. 영작문 클리닉

8 상황별 부사의 쓰임

1. 단정을 의미할 때

certainly, definitely, clearly, actually, undoubtedly,

2. 짐작을 의미할 때

perhaps, probably, likely, presumably, possibly

3. 앞의 말에 대한 결과를 의미할 때

therefore, accordingly, consequently, so, as a result, thus, hence

4. 덧붙일 때

also, in addition, moreover, furthermore, additionally, above all

5. 요약이나 결론을 유도할 때

in conclusion, to conclude, in brief, therefore,

6. 앞서 말한 것을 다시 언급할 때

that is, that is to say, in other words, i.e

7. 앞의 것과 대조를 이룰 때

conversely, by contrast, however, while, on the contrary, on the other hand, although, nevertheless, nonetheless, instead, yet, in spite of, despite, even if

9 틀리기 쉬운 영작문형

1. **Someone hit me on the head.** (누군가가 나의 머리를 때렸다.)
    ▶ 신체의 일부를 나타내는 부분과 동사의 결합은,
      〈hit (pat) + 사람(목적어) + 전치사(on) + the + 신체의 일부〉의 패턴을 취한다.
      • They hit him **on** the face.
    cf) She pulled me **by** the sleeve. (take · pull은 on과 함께 쓰인다.)
         He looked him **in** the face. (look은 in과 함께 쓰인다.)

2. **Neither** my sister **nor** my brothers **want** to work in an office.
    (나의 누이도 나의 형제도 사무실에서 일하는 것을 좋아하지 않는다.)
    ▶ 〈Neither A nor B〉는 B에 동사를 일치한다.

3. **A number of** items **have** been deleted. (수많은 항목들이 삭제되었다.)
    ▶ 〈a number of〉는 동사가 복수 취급을 한다.

4. **The number of** deleted items **is** small. (삭제된 항목들의 수는 적다.)
    ▶ 〈The number of〉는 동사가 단수 취급을 한다.

5. **I persuaded** my father **to** lend me the money.
    (나는 나의 아버지가 내게 돈을 빌려주게 설득했다.)
    ▶ want · expect · decide · persuade 등과 같이 〈to부정사 구문〉을 취하는 동사를 익혀야 한다.

6. **Sue is accustomed to working** long hours.
    (Sue는 오랜 시간 동안 일하는 데 익숙하다.)
    ▶ 전치사 뒤에 나오는 동사형은 동명사를 취하며, enjoy · mind · finish · avoid · consider · deny 등과 같이 목적어로 동명사를 취하는 동사에 유의한다.

7. **I have no intention of driving** to Nevada.
    (나는 네바다로 운전해 갈 의도가 없다.)
    ▶ 전치사 of의 목적어로 동명사 driving이 쓰였다.

8. **Had I gone** to the postoffice, **I would have bought** stamps.
   (만약 내가 우체국에 갔었다면, 나는 우표를 샀을 텐데)
   - ▶ 영어의 가정법구문에서 if가 생략되면 주어와 동사의 어순이 바뀐다.
     이 문장은 원래 다음의 문장이 된다:
     = If I had gone to the postoffice, I would have bought stamps.

9. **Never** again **did Max** buy another motorcycle.
   (Max는 결코 다시는 다른 오토바이를 사지 않았다.)
   - ▶ 문장의 앞에 부정어(never · only · not 등)가 오거나, 부사어가 오면 주어와 동사의 어순이 바뀐다.

10. **Not only does Mary** work at the postoffice, **but** she **also** works at the grocery store.
    (메리는 우체국에서 일할 뿐만 아니라, 식료품 가게에서도 일한다.)
    - ▶ 문장 앞에 부정어나 부사어가 오면 주절의 주어와 동사는 도치된다:
      〈Not only〉가 문두에 오므로 〈does + Mary〉의 도치형이 되었다.

11. **Only** once every seventy-six years **does Halley's** comet appear in the sky.
    (76년에 한번만 헬리 혜성은 하늘에 나타난다.)
    - ▶ 〈Only ~ years〉라는 부정적 부사절이 앞에 오므로 〈does + Halley's comet〉라는 도치구문을 이루고 있다.

12. I had two peaches. I ate **one** and put **the other** in a bowl.
    (나는 복숭아가 2개 있다. 나는 하나를 먹고 나머지는 그릇에 넣었다.)
    - ▶ 2개의 내용을 설명할 때 하나는 one, 나머지 하나는 the other이다.

13. It is easy to understand why **fast-food restaurants are so popular**.
    (패스트푸드 레스토랑이 아주 인기가 있는 것을 이해하기는 쉽다.)
    - ▶ 주어가 긴 경우에는 가주어 it을 사용하여 쓴다. why 이하가 진주어가 된다.

14. The man **whom** we saw works nearby.
    (우리가 보았던 그 사람은 근처에서 일한다.)
    - ▶ 관계대명사를 이용한 형용사절 구문은 관계대명사절이 앞의 명사를 수식한다.
      whom we saw가 the man을 수식하고 있다.

15. The school **where** I met my husband is now closed.
    (내가 나의 남편을 만났던 학교는 지금 닫혀있다.)
    - ▶ 관계부사를 이용한 형용사절이 앞의 명사를 수식한다. where I met my husband가 the school을 수식한다.

16. The writer published a book **containing** illustrations.
    (작가는 삽화가 포함되어 있는 책을 출판했다.)
    - ▶ 분사는 명사 앞, 뒤에서 수식하는 기능이 있다. containing이 a book을 수식한다.

17. The magazine ad, **which was printed in Times Weekly**, showed the city skyline.
    (Times Weekly에 나왔던 잡지 광고는 도시의 스카이라인을 보여주었다.)
    - ▶ 문장 중간에 있는 관계사절은 양쪽에 콤마(,)를 찍으며, 앞의 명사를 수식한다.

18. The ideas **presented** in the previous meeting were discussed.
    (그 전 미팅에서 제시됐던 아이디어들이 토론되었다.)
    - ▶ 과거분사 presented가 앞의 명사 the ideas를 수식한다. 이 문장은 원래 The ideas which was presented in the previous meeting were discussed.가 된다.

19. The woman **whose son** is blocking the entrance works upstairs.
    (입구를 막고 있는 아들을 둔 그 여자는 2층에서 일한다.)
    - ▶ 관계대명사 소유격은 뒤의 명사를 수반하며 형용사절 역할을 한다.

20. Betty looks **as if she knew everything**.
    (베티는 마치 모든 것을 아는것 처럼 보인다.)
    - ▶ as if 뒤에는 가정법 구문이 오므로 동사는 과거형(가정법 과거)이나 과거완료 〈had + P.P〉(가정법 과거완료) 형이 나온다.

21. We can go camping with Bill **Provided** we bring our own equipment.
    (우리가 우리 자신의 장비를 가져온다면, 빌과 함께 캠핑갈 수 있다.)
    - ▶ 조건절의 대용으로 provided (providing) · in case · given 등을 사용하기도 한다.

22. Lucy can't attend the meeting **unless** she finds a baby-sitter.
    (루시가 아기 보는 사람을 찾지 않는다면, 회의에 참석할 수 없다.)
    - ▶ unless는 〈if ~ not〉의 의미로 부정 조건문을 보여줄 때 쓰인다.

23. **Despite the fact that** she was ill, Lisa went on stage.
    (그녀가 아프다는 사실에도 불구하고, 리사는 무대 위에 올랐다.)
    - ▶ 양보절을 나타내는 패턴 중 〈despite〉와 〈in spite of〉는 〈~에도 불구하고〉라는 의미로 쓰인다.

24. That was **the most** convincing movie I've ever seen.
    (저것은 내가 지금까지 본 것 중에서 가장 감동적인 영화였다.)
    - ▶ 최상급 구문은 〈the + most + 명사 +~ ever〉의 패턴을 취한다.

25. **The more** encouragement he got, **the harder** she tried to succeed.
    (그가 격려를 많이 받으면 받을수록, 더 열심히 성공하려고 노력했다.)
    - ▶ 〈the more …… the more〉 구문은 〈~하면 할수록 그 만큼 ~하다〉의 의미로 쓰인다.

26. **Reading, writing, and calculating** are important skills to learn.
    (읽기, 쓰기, 계산하기는 배우기 위한 중요한 기술들이다.)
    - ▶ 병렬구문은 등위접속사 and를 중심으로 같은 품사(동명사)로 쓴다.

27. After her accident, Emma had to learn **how to** speak, **to** walk, and **to** write again.
    (엠마는 사고 후에 말하고, 걷고, 쓰는 법을 다시 배워야 했다.)
    - ▶ 병렬구조로 동사 learn의 목적어로, and를 중심으로 how to 이하가 to부정사 구조로 연결되고 있다.

28. The creation of a map is a compromise of **what need to be done** and **what we would like to include**.
    (지도의 탄생은 할 필요가 있는 것과 우리가 포함시키고자 하는 것과의 절충이다.)
    - ▶ 병렬구문으로 전치사 of의 목적어로 what절과 what절이 and를 중심으로 연결되고 있다.

29. Money is required for research to **advance**.
    (돈은 실험이 발전하기 위해 꼭 필요한 것이다.)
    - ▶ 영어의 중복구문에서는 불필요한 표현을 반복하지 않는다. 이 문장에서는 Money is required for research to advance forward.라고 쓰지 않는다.

30. The tourist industry has **expanded** in recent years.
    (관광산업은 최근에 팽창되었다.)
    - ▶ 이 문장은 중복구문으로 The tourist industry has expanded for longer time in recent years.라고 쓰지 않는다.

31. Korean kids are left unchecked while being provided with almost everything they want, thus **becoming** more dependent on their parents.
    (한국 아이들은 그들이 원하는 거의 모든 것을 제공 받았을 때, 무방비로 남는다. 그래서 부모에게 점점 의존하게 된다.)
    - ▶ 분사구문의 동시상황을 설명하는 구문으로 〈thus becoming more dependent on~〉은 〈and thus become more dependent on~〉과 같은 의미이다. 분사구문은 접속사의 의미와 시제를 함께 내포하고 있는 구문이다.

10. 영작문 필수구문 정리

1. seem to (appear to) : ~처럼 보이다
happen to : 우연히 ~하다

- It seems that he is ill.
    = He seems to be ill.
- It happens that I have no money with me.
    = I happen to have no money.

작문연습

주어진 표현을 이용하여 영작하시오.

① 그는 그 결과에 만족하지 않는 것처럼 보인다. (appear to / be dissatisfied with)

2. keep (hold · remain) + 형용사, 전치사구 : ~한 상태로 만들다

- I keep in good condition.
- The weather holds chilly.

작문연습

주어진 표현을 이용하여 영작하시오.

② 그는 결혼 하지 않은 채 있다. (remain / unmarried)

모범답안

① He appears (to be) dissatisfied with the result.
② He remained unmarried.

I. 영작문 클리닉

3. sound · feel · smell · taste · look + 형용사 :
~하게 들리다 · 느끼다 · 냄새나다 · 맛나다 · 보이다

- The food smells good.
- The plan sounds feasible.
- The music sounds sweet.

작문연습

주어진 표현을 이용하여 영작하시오.

③ 그는 행복해 보인다. (look / happy)

④ 그것은 부드럽게 느껴진다. (feel / smooth)

4. 재귀목적어

- People often hurt **themselves** by hurting nature.
- She absented **herself** from school yesterday.
- He presented **himself** at the meeting.

작문연습

주어진 표현을 이용하여 영작하시오.

⑤ 그들은 그 기회를 이용했다. (avail / opportunity)

⑥ 그는 자기의 부(재산)를 자랑했다. (pride / wealth)

모범답안

③ He looks happy.
④ It feels smooth.
⑤ They availed themselves of that opportunity.
⑥ He prided himself on his wealth.

5. 5형식 구문 : 주어 + 동사 + 목적어 + 목적격 보어 (명사·대명사·형용사·부정사)

- We call him Little Jack.
- President appointed him minister of foreign affairs.
- We kept the window closed.

작문연습

주어진 표현을 이용하여 영작하시오.

⑦ 찬바람이 나뭇잎들을 붉고 노랗게 변하게 했다. (cold wind / turn)

⑧ 그는 나를 홀로 놔두지 않았다. (leave / alone)

⑨ 우리는 방이 빈 것을 발견했다. (find / empty)

영·작·특·강 — 주요 5형식 구문

1. 보어가 to 부정사

- She compelled her son to attend the party.
  (compel A to B = A가 B 하도록 강요하다)
- We want you to come tomorrow.
- Much money enabled him to study abroad.
  (enable A to B = A가 B를 할 수 있게 하다)
- The general ordered his men to move on.
- I persuaded her not to go to the party.
  (persuade A to B = A가 B 하도록 설득하다)

모범답안

⑦ The cold wind turned the leaves red and yellow.   ⑧ He doesn't leave me alone.
⑨ We found the room empty.

작문연습 주어진 표현을 이용하여 영작하시오.

① 그 아이는 자기 아빠에게 오늘 밤 영화 보러 가자고 부탁했다.
(ask / go to the movies)

....

② 그의 긴 편지가 그녀로 하여금 마음을 바꾸도록 만들었다.
(cause~ to / change one's mind)

....

2. 보어가 원형부정사

(1) 사역동사 뒤에
- He **had** me **build** the house.
- Please **let** me **know** what to do.

(2) 지각동사 뒤에
- I **saw** him **swim** in the river.
- She could **feel** her heart **beat**.

작문연습 주어진 표현을 이용하여 영작하시오.

③ 너는 Jack이 그 집을 떠난다는 것을 들었니? (hear / leave)

....

④ 나는 어떤 사람이 그 집에 들어가는 것을 알아차렸다. (notice / enter)

....

3. 보어가 현재분사(목적어가 동작을 나타낼 때)

- The teacher found a pupil **dozing**.
- Don't leave the baby **crying**.

작문연습 주어진 표현을 이용하여 영작하시오.

⑤ 나는 너를 계속 기다리게 해서 미안하다. (sorry / keep / wait)

....

4. 보어가 과거분사 (목적어가 수동이나 상태를 나타낼 때)

- She found the jewel **gone**.
- I had my house **built** by the workers.
- I got my trousers **lengthened** by my mother.
- I couldn't make myself **understood** in English.

작문연습 주어진 표현을 이용하여 영작하시오.

⑥ 나는 내일까지 그 일이 끝나기를 바란다. (want / job / do)

⑦ 나는 이발을 해야 한다. (have one's hair cut)

모범답안
① The child asked his father to go the movies tonight.
② His long letter caused her to change her mind.
③ Did you hear Jack leave the house?
④ I noticed a man enter the house.
⑤ I'm sorry to have kept you waiting.
⑥ I want the job done by tomorrow.
⑦ I must have my hair cut.

6. 어순 도치 구문 : 부정을 나타내는 부사 never · little · seldom 등을 문두에 놓을 때 주어와 동사는 도치된다.

- Never **did I** think of it.
- Little **did she** dream that he was alive.

작문연습 주어진 표현을 이용하여 영작하시오.

⑩ 내가 그녀를 공원에서 만날 거라고 꿈에도 생각하지 않았다. (little / dream)

모범답안
⑩ Little did I dream that I met her in the park.

I. 영작문 클리닉

7. 양보의 부사절 : 비록 ~일지라도, ~일지 모르겠지만

① wh-ever + S + may + 원형~
② No matter wh-ever + S + may + 원형~,
③ 형용사, 분사, 부사, 무관사 명사 + as + S + (may) + 원형~

- **Wherever you may go,** I will follow you.
  = No matter where you may go, I will follow you.
- **However humble it may be,** there is no place like home.
- **Woman as she is,** she is very bold.

작문연습

주어진 표현을 이용하여 영작하시오.

⑪ 어디에 가든 너는 그 책을 찾을 수 없다. (wherever / may)

⑫ 우리가 그것을 어떻게 하든, 그것은 잘못일 것이다. (however / wrong)

8. should have + P.P = ought to have P.P : ~했어야만 했는데(실제로는 하지 않았다)

- You **should have driven** more carefully.

작문연습

주어진 표현을 이용하여 영작하시오.

⑬ 콘서트는 성공적이었다. 너는 우리와 함께 왔어야 했는데. (concert / should)

모범답안

⑪ Wherever you may go, you can't find the book.
⑫ However we do it, it will be wrong.
⑬ The concert was successful. You should have come with us.

9. 조동사 should의 특수 구문

〈의향〉의 should
〈요구·주장·제안·소망·필요·명령·충고〉 등의 의향을 나타내는 동사에 계속되는 명사절(that절) 안에 should를 쓴다. 또는 should를 생략하고 원형만 쓰기도 한다.

- He insisted that he (should) go to the party.
- He ordered that the boy (should) be sent to the town alone.
- My wife demanded that I (should) never leave her alone.
- The ambassador requested that the captured ships (should) be returned.
- I move that the case (should) be adjourned till tomorrow.

작문연습

주어진 표현을 이용하여 영작하시오.

⑭ 그는 죄수가 석방되어야 한다고 명령했다. (command / prisoner / should / release)

⑮ 그녀는 우리가 하룻밤 더 머무르기를 제안했다. (propose / should / stay / another)

이성적 판단의 should
It is + necessary · important · natural · desirable · right · wrong · essential + (that) + S + should + 원형

- It is natural that he should get angry with you.
    = It is natural for him to get angry with you.
    It is necessary that you should be present at the meeting.

작문연습

주어진 표현을 이용하여 영작하시오.

⑯ 그 사람이 직업을 구하는 것은 중요하다. (important / should / get a job)

모범답안
⑭ He commanded that the prisoner (should) be released.　⑮ She proposed that we (should) stay another night.
⑯ It is important that the man should get a job.

감정(성)적 판단의 should
It is + a pity · surprising · regrettable · strange · odd (that) + S + should + 원형

- It is a pity that Tom **should** lose his wallet.
- It is surprising that she **should** have killed herself.

작문연습

주어진 표현을 이용하여 영작하시오.

⑰ 그 아이가 너무 약한 것은 유감이다. (regrettable / should / weak)

⑱ 네가 그것에 대해 잘 모르는 것은 이상하다. (strange / should)

10. 목적을 나타내는 부사절

lest · for fear + S + should + 원형 : ~하지 않도록

- We hid behind the trees lest they should see us.
  = We hid behind the trees for fear (that) they should see us.
- I hid it carefully for fear the children should see.

작문연습

주어진 표현을 이용하여 영작하시오.

⑲ 나는 그 아이가 물을 마시지 않도록 물을 치워 버렸다. (take away / lest ~ should)

모범답안
⑰ It was regrettable that the child should be so weak.   ⑱ It is strange that you should know so little about it.
⑲ I took away the water lest the child should drink it.

11. used to

(1) 과거의 습관
- When I was a child, I used to [would] get up early.

(2) 과거의 상태
- There used to be a pond here.

(3) 혼동하기 쉬운 표현

> be used to + 원형 : ~하기 위해 사용된다
> be used to + -ing / 명사 : ~에 익숙하다

- Dictionaries are used to look up the words you don't know.
- She is used to singing before large audiences.

작문연습

주어진 표현을 이용하여 영작하시오.

⑳ 나는 대중 앞에서 이야기하는 데 익숙하다. (be accustomed to / in public)

㉑ 그녀는 많은 청중 앞에서 노래하곤 했다. (use to / large audiences)

12. 양보 명령

> 동사원형 + as절 ~ = However + 형용사, 부사 + S + may + 원형 ~
> = No matter how + 형용사, 부사 + S + may + 원형~

- Try hard as you may, you can't pass the test.
  = However hard you may try, you can't pass the test.

모범답안

⑳ I am accustomed to speaking in public.
㉑ She used to sing before large audiences.

작문연습 주어진 표현을 이용하여 영작하시오.

㉒ 너는 아무리 열심히 노력을 해도 그 시험을 통과할 수 없다. (no matter how ~ may)

....

> 동사원형 + S + ever so + 형용사 : ~아무리 ~한다 해도
> = However + 형용사 + S + may + 원형~
> = No matter how + 형용사 + S + may + 원형~

- Be it ever so humble, there is no place like home.
  = However humble it may be, there is no place like home.

작문연습 주어진 표현을 이용하여 영작하시오.

㉓ 아무리 초라해도 자기 집 같은 곳은 없다. (no matter how humble ~ may)

....

> 명령문 + A or B ~ (= Whether~)

- Be it true or not, it is not worth considering.
  = Whether it is true or not, it is not worth considering.

> 기타 let alone : ~은 말할 것도 없이
>   say : 가령, 말하자면
>   suppose : 만약 ~ 한다면

- He cannot speak English, **let alone** French.
- Come and see me one of these days, **say**, next Sunday
- **Suppose** you fail, what will you do?

모범답안
㉒ No matter how hard you may try, you can't pass the test.
㉓ No matter how humble it may be, there is no place like home.

13. 가정법 과거

If + S + 과거동사 ~, S + 조동사의 과거형 + 원형 ~ :
만일 ~한다면, ~할 텐데

- If I **knew** her name, I **would** tell you.
- If it **were** not raining, I **would** play tennis.

작문연습

주어진 표현을 이용하여 영작하시오.

㉔ 만약 내가 날개가 있다면 너에게 날아갈 텐데. (if / fly)

....

14. 가정법 과거완료

If + S + had + P.P ~, S + would, should, + have + P.P ··· :
만약 ~했더라면, ··· 했을 텐데

- If he **had tried** harder last week, he **would have passed** the test.
- If you **had left** earlier, you **could have caught** the train.

작문연습

주어진 표현을 이용하여 영작하시오.

㉕ 만약 네가 나를 돕지 않았었다면 나는 실패했을 것이다. (if / help / fail)

....

모범답안

㉔ If I had wings, I would[could] fly to you.
㉕ If you had not helped me, I should have failed.

15. I wish나 as if가 이끄는 절의 시제의 일치

I wish + 가정법 : ~이기를 바랬는데

- I wish I **were** rich.
- I wished I **were** rich.

as if + 가정법 : 마치 ~인 것처럼 ~하다

- He talks as if he **were** rich.
- He talks as if he **had been** rich.
- He talked as if he **were** rich.
- He talked as if he **had been** rich.

16. 가정법을 포함하는 특수 구문 (조건절의 대용)

It is (high) time (that) + S + 과거 V (가정법 과거) ~ : ~해야 할 시간(때)다

- It is time that you went to bed.
  = It is time that you should go to bed.
  = It is time for you to go to bed.

If it were not for ~ : 만약 (지금) ~이 없다면 …할 텐데

- If it were not for air, we should die.
  = But for air, we should die.
  = Without air, we should die.
  = Were it not for air, we should die.

작문연습 주어진 표현을 이용하여 영작하시오.

㉖ 만약 너의 도움이 없다면 나는 그것을 할 수 없을 것이다. (if it were not for)

㉗ 만약 태양이 없다면 아무것도 지구상에 살 수 없을 것이다. (if it were not for)

모범답안
㉖ If it were not for your help, I could not do it.
㉗ If it were not for the sun, nothing could live on the earth.

cf) **If it had not been for** his advice, I should have failed.
(그의 충고가 없었더라면 나는 실패했을 텐데.) (가정법 과거완료)

17. if절 대신 사용할 수 있는 구문

In case (that) / In case of + 명사 :
 ~할 경우에는, 만약~한다면, ~의 경우에 대비하여

- Take an umbrella with you **in case it** should (may) rain.
  = Take an umbrella **in the event of** rain.
  In case of trouble, call for my help.

On condition (that) : 만약 ~하기만 하면, ~라는 조건으로

- I will accept the post **on condition that** you assist me.

Granted [Granting] (that) : 양보 〈만약 ~한다 할지라도〉 = even if

- **Granted that** it is true, it doesn't matter to me.
- **Granting** it to be true, how do you explain this?

18. If의 생략

if절에서 if를 생략하고 조동사(동사)를 문두에 두고
주어, 동사를 도치시켜서 도치구문으로 할 수 있다.

(1) 가정법 과거:
- If I were you, I would try again. = Were I you, I would try again.
- If she were my wife, I should be happy.
  = Were

  (모범영작) she my wife, I should be happy.

- If I possessed the book, I would lend it to you.
  = Did

  (모범영작) I possess the book, I would lend it to you.

작문연습 주어진 표현을 이용하여 영작하시오.

㉘ 너의 도움이 없다면 나는 그 일을 끝낼 수 없을 것이다. (were it not for)

....

(2) 가정법 과거완료
- If I had tried harder, I could have passed the exam.
    = Had I tried harder, I could have passed the exam.
- If he had known it in time, he would not have made the mistakes.

    = Had ....

(모범영작) he known it, he would not have made the mistakes.

(3) 가정법 미래
- If it should be fine tomorrow, I will play tennis.
    = Should it be fine tomorrow, I will play tennis.
- If you should want to contact me, call this number.

    = Should ....

(모범영작) you want to contact me, call this number.

19. 목적어가 명사절(that절)인 경우

- I request that she (should) be sent home.
    → It is requested that she (should) be sent home.
- They say that he is rich.
    → It is said that he is rich = He is said to be rich.
- They say that he was rich.

    → It is said ....

(모범영작) that he was rich.

- He is said ....

(모범영작) to have been rich.

모범답안   ㉘ Were it not for your help, I could not finish the work.

20. 경험의 수동태 : S + have [get] + O + p.p.

(1) 사역의 뜻
- I had [got] my audio mended. = My audio was mended.

(2) 수동의 뜻
- I had [got] my purse stolen. = My purse was stolen. purse.

21. it is ~ for 의미상의 주어 + to + 원형

It is difficult 〈hard · possible · impossible · natural · important · essential〉 for ~ to

- It is difficult for Tom to master Korean.
- It is dangerous for Tom to swim in this river. (O)
    → Tom is dangerous to swim in this river. (X)

22. 완료부정사 : to have + p.p.

주절(본동사)의 시제보다 that절(종속절)의 동사의 시제가 하나 앞선(그 이전) 시제를 나타낸다.

- He seems to have been rich.
    = It seems that he was[has been] rich.
- He seemed to have been rich.
    = It seemed that

(모범영작) he had been rich.

23. 동명사 용법

전치사의 목적어가 된다 : 전치사 다음에 오는 동사는 동명사로 해야 한다.

- She is fond of **playing** the piano.
- Don't be afraid of **making** mistakes.
- He punished me for **being** late.

24. 동명사의 의미상의 주어를 표시하는 경우

동명사의 의미상의 주어는 (대)명사의 〈소유격〉을 원칙으로 한다.

- I have no objection to **his** [**Tom's**] going there.
- I am sure of **his** succeeding.
- I am afraid of **her** coming late.
- He insisted on **my** going there.

작문연습 주어진 표현을 이용하여 영작하시오.

㉙ 그녀는 그가 그녀에게 다시 돌아올 것을 의심하지 않는다. (have no doubt of)

㉚ 너는 내가 여기서 담배 피워도 괜찮니? (mind / smoke)

동명사의 의미상의 주어가 무생물일 경우는 일반적으로 〈목적격〉으로 나타낸다.

- We must allow for **the train** being late.

25. 현재분사

동사 + ing (동작동사) : ~하고 있는 (능동, 진행의 의미)

- Look at the **singing** bird
- The bird **singing** on the tree is a lark.
- Who is that **running** boy?

작문연습 주어진 표현을 이용하여 영작하시오.

㉛ 도시에 사는 사람들은 매일 아주 바쁘다. (live / busy)

모범답안
㉙ She has no doubt of his coming back to her.
㉚ Do you mind my smoking here?
㉛ People living in cities are very busy everyday.

26. 과거분사

~한, 해버린 : 동작이 완료된 결과, 상태를 의미

- My garden is **filled** with fallen leaves
- He threw out the **faded** flowers.
- He is a **returned** soldier

작문연습

주어진 표현을 이용하여 영작하시오.

㉜ 운동장 위에 떨어져 있는 나뭇잎은 그 노인에 의해 치워졌다. (leaves/ fall /ground/ clean)

㉝ 치과의사가 썩은 이를 뽑았다. (dentist / pull out / decay / tooth)

cf) 타동사의 과거분사 : ~해진, 되어진, ~당한, 받은 (수동적 의미)

- Three wounded soldier were **taken** to the hospital.
- I am going to buy a **used** car.
- He has a lovely daughter **called** Betty.
- a door **locked** from the inside

27. With + (대)명사 [O] + 분사형의 분사구문

(부대상황) ~을 한 채로, …을 ~하며, ~을 하면서

- I fell asleep **with the TV turned on**.
- It was a calm morning, **with little wind blowing**.

작문연습

주어진 표현을 이용하여 영작하시오.

㉞ 그는 산책을 나갔고 그의 개는 그를 따라갔다. (go for a walk / with / follow)

모범답안

㉜ The leaves fallen on the ground were cleaned by the old man.　㉝ The dentist pulled out a decayed tooth.
㉞ He went for a walk, with his dog following him.

with + O (목적어) + 부사(구)

- What a lonely world it would be **with you away**!
  = What a lonely world it would be if you are away.
  He stood there with his spectacles on [off].

- with one's hat on(off) 모자를 쓰고서
- with a pipe in one's mouth 입에 파이프를 물고

with + O (목적어) + 형용사

- Don't speak **with your mouth full**.
- She went out **with her room empty**.
- Don't leave the room **with the window open**.

28. 복수형이 단수 취급을 받는 경우

(1) 수사 + 〈시간 · 거리 · 금액 · 무게〉의 복수명사가 하나의 단일 단위(관념)를 나타내는 경우
- Ten miles is a long distance to me.

작문연습 주어진 표현을 이용하여 영작하시오.

㉟ 10년은 해외에서 살기에 아주 긴 시간이다. (live abroad)

(2) 복수형 학과명 · 국명 · news · 병명 등
- Mathematics is a very interesting subject.

작문연습 주어진 표현을 이용하여 영작하시오.

㊱ 미국은 자원이 풍부하다. (rich / resources)

모범답안
㉟ Ten years is a very long time to live abroad.
㊱ The United States is rich in resources.

29. 주의해야 할 일치의 법칙

(1) A or B : 〈A 또는 B〉 : B에 동사를 일치시킨다

• He or you **are** in the wrong.

(2) either A or B : 〈A 또는 B 둘 중 하나〉 : B에 동사를 일치시킨다

• Either John or you **are** in the wrong.

(3) neither A nor B : 〈A도 B도 ~아니다〉 : B에 일치시킨다

• Neither you nor he **was** wrong.

= Neither you (were wrong) nor he was wrong.

(4) not only A but (also) B = B as well as A : 〈A뿐만 아니라 B도〉 : B에 일치시킨다

• Not only the passengers but also the driver **was** killed.

= The driver as well as the passengers was killed.

30. a number of + 복수 명사 + 복수 동사: 많은 ~ the number of + 복수 명사 + 단수 동사 : ~의 수

• A number of the students in our class **are** absent.
• The number of the students in our class **is** fifty.

31. as를 사용한 양보절

형용사 · 분사 · 부사 · 무관사 명사 + as + S + (may) + R ~ = though + S + V ~

• **Woman as she is**, she is very bold.

작문연습

주어진 표현을 이용하여 영작하시오.

㊲ 그녀는 부자이지만, 만족하지 않았다. (as / content)

모범답안

㊲ Rich as she was, she was not contented.

32. scarcely A when [before] B : A 하자마자 B 하다

S + had + scarcely + P.P.(A) ~ when [before · hardly] + S' + 과거 V(B) …

- **Scarcely had he** gone out **when** it began to rain.

작문연습

주어진 표현을 이용하여 영작하시오.

㊳ 내가 잠들자마자, 나는 깨어났다. (scarcely~ before / fall asleep / awake)

모범답안

㊳ I had scarcely fallen asleep before I was awakened.

영작문 클리닉 연습

1. 그는 아픈 것처럼 보인다. (seem to)

2. 그는 결혼하지 않은 상태로 남아 있다. (remain)

3. 나는 좋은 상태를 유지하고 있다. (keep)

4. 너는 나의 입장을 이해할 수 없는 것처럼 보였다. (seem)

5. 그는 그 결과에 불만족 하는 것처럼 보인다. (appear)

6. 그 음악은 달콤하게 들린다. (sound)

7. 그들은 저 기회를 이용했다. (avail oneself of)

8. 그녀는 어제 학교에 결석했다. (absent)

9. 대통령은 그를 외무부 장관으로 임명했다. (appoint)

10. 찬바람이 나뭇잎들을 붉고 노랗게 만들었다. (turn)

11. 우리는 그 방이 텅 빈 것을 알았다. (find)

12. 그녀는 그녀의 아들을 파티에 참석하도록 강요했다. (compel)

13. 그는 많은 돈 때문에 해외에서 공부할 수 있었다. (enable)

14. 내가 무엇을 해야 할지 알려주세요. (let)

15. 너는 Jack이 집을 떠난다는 것을 들었니? (hear)

16. 그녀는 그녀의 마음이 뛰는 것을 느낄 수 있었다. (feel)

17. 내가 당신을 계속 기다리게 해서 미안합니다. (keep)

18. 나는 그녀가 파티에 가지 말도록 설득했다. (persuade)

19. 아기가 울도록 놓아두지 마세요. (leave)

20. 나는 나의 집을 그 일꾼들에 의해서 지어지도록 만들었다. (have + 목적어 + P.P)

21. 나는 영어로 의사소통을 할 수 없었다. (make oneself understood)

22. 나는 이발을 해야만 한다. (have + 목적어 + P.P)

23. 네가 어디에 있다 하더라도, 나는 너를 따라갈 것이다. (no matter where)

24. 네가 아무리 열심히 노력한다 해도, 시험에 합격할 수 없다. (no matter how)

25. 아무리 초라하다 하더라도 자기 집만한 곳은 없다. (be it ever so)

26. 그것이 사실이건 아니건 간에, 고려할 가치가 없다. (whether ~ or not)

27. 그는 불어는 말할 것도 없이, 영어를 말할 수 없다. (let alone)

28. 만약 내가 그녀의 이름을 안다면, 너에게 말해주겠다. (가정법 과거)

29. 만약 네가 좀더 일찍 떠났었더라면, 너는 기차를 잡을 수 있었을 텐데. (가정법 과거완료)

30. 내가 부자라면 좋겠는데. (I wish)

31. 너는 좀더 조심스럽게 운전해야 했을 텐데. (should have P.P)

32. 그는 그 아이를 혼자 그 도시로 보내라고 명령했다. (order)

33. 그녀는 우리가 하룻밤 더 머물 것을 제안했다. (propose)

34. 그가 너에게 화내는 것은 당연하다. (natural)

35. Tom이 그의 지갑을 잃어버린 것은 유감이다. (pity)

36. 네가 그 점에 대하여 그렇게 잘 알지 못하는 것은 이상하다. (strange)

37. 나는 그 아이가 그것을 마시지 못하도록 물을 치웠다. (lest ~ should)

38. 내가 어린 아이였을 때 일찍 일어나곤 했다. (used to)

39. 그녀는 많은 청중 앞에서 노래하는 데 익숙하다. (be used to ~ing)

40. 그는 마치 부자였었던 것처럼 말한다. (as if)

41. 네가 잠자리에 들 시간이다. (it is time)

42. 너의 도움이 없다면 그 일을 할 수 없을 텐데. (if it were not for)

43. 나는 그의 충고가 없었더라면, 실패했을 텐데. (if it had not been for)

44. 너는 비가 올 경우에 우산을 가져가라. (in case)

45. 다른 모든 사람들이 동의한다면, 나는 승낙할 것이다. (provided)

46. 만약 내일 날씨가 좋다면, 테니스를 칠 것이다. (should)

47. 그가 부자라고들 한다. (it is said)

48. 나는 나의 지갑을 잃어버렸다. (have + 목적어 + P.P)

49. 인생에서 가장 중요한 것은 어떻게 사느냐 하는 것이다. (how to)

50. 너는 그 주제에 대하여 무슨 말을 해야 하는지 아느냐? (what to)

51. Tom이 한국어를 마스터하는 것은 어렵다. (difficult)

52. Tom이 이 강에서 수영하는 것은 위험하다. (dangerous)

53. 그는 부자였던 것처럼 보인다. (seem to)

54. 나는 시험에 합격할 수 있도록 열심히 공부했다. (so that)

55. 나는 그에게 세차하라고 시킬 것이다. (have + 사람 + 원형)

56. 나는 나의 차를 수리했다. (have + 목적어 + P.P)

57. 나를 파티에 초대해 주어 고맙다. (thank)

58. 나는 그가 그곳에 가는 것을 반대하지 않는다. (objection)

59. 그는 내가 그곳에 가는 것을 주장하고 있다. (insist on)

60. 내가 여기서 담배를 피워도 됩니까? (mind)

61. 그녀는 밖에 나가는 대신 집에 머물렀다. (instead of)

62. 네가 왜 그것을 했는지 한 가지 이유를 말해라. (reason why)

63. 도시에 사는 사람들은 매일 아주 바쁘다. (live in)

64. 나무 위에서 노래하는 새는 종달새다. (sing)

65. 나의 정원은 낙엽으로 가득 찼다. (be filled with)

66. 땅 위에 떨어져 있는 나뭇잎들은 그 노인에 의해 치워졌다. (fall)

67. 3명의 부상병들은 병원으로 옮겨졌다. (wound)

68. 그는 Betty라고 불리우는 사랑스런 딸을 갖고 있다. (call)

69. 그 노인은 만족스럽게 보였다. (satisfy)

70. 나는 그녀가 방 안에서 울고 있는 것을 발견했다. (weep)

71. 나는 무언가가 나의 등을 건드리는 것을 느꼈다. (touch)

72. 나는 나 자신이 항상 감시당하는 것을 느꼈다. (watch)

73. 나는 그 일꾼들이 그 집을 짓도록 시켰다. (have + 목적어 + P.P)

74. 나는 산책하러 나갔고, 그의 개는 그를 따라가고 있었다.
(with + 목적어 + 동사 ~ing)

75. 나는 TV를 켜고서 잠이 들었다. (with + 목적어 + P.P)

76. 비는 내내 내렸고, 우리의 휴일을 완전히 망가뜨리고 있었다. (completely ruin)

77. 그는 벽에 머리를 기대고 서 있었다. (with + 목적어 + 동사 ~ ing)

78. 그는 다리를 포개고 의자에 앉았다. (with + 목적어 + P.P)

79. 그는 팔짱을 끼고서 나무 밑에 앉았다. (with + 목적어 + P.P)

80. 그는 안경을 끼고서 그 곳에 서 있었다. (with + 목적어 + on)

81. 그녀는 방을 텅 빈 상태로 하고 밖으로 나갔다. (with)

82. 10년은 외국에서 살기에 매우 긴 시간이다. (live abroad)

83. 수학은 매우 재미있는 과목이다. (mathematics)

84. 청중들은 매우 감동 받았다. (move)

85. John이나 너 가운데 한 명이 잘못이다. (either ~ or)

86. 너나 그 중에 한 명도 잘못이 없다. (neither ~ nor)

87. 승객들뿐만 아니라 운전기사도 죽었다. (not only ~ but also)

88. 우리 학급 학생들의 수는 50명이다. (the number of)

89. 우리 학급의 많은 학생들이 결석이다. (a number of)

90. 그녀는 부자였지만 만족하지 않았다. (형용사 + as + 주어 + 동사)

91. 우리가 높이 올라갈수록 날씨는 추워진다. (the 비교급, the 비교급)

92. 우리가 열심히 하면 할수록 그만큼 우리 자신이 무지한 것을 알게 된다.
(the 비교급, the 비교급)

93. 우리는 건강을 잃고서 비로소 그 가치를 알게 된다. (not ~ until)

94. 그가 밖에 나가자마자 비가 오기 시작했다. (scarcely ~ when)

95. 그는 그의 부에 대해 자부심을 갖고 있다. (pride oneself on)

96. 그는 젊지만 매우 조심스럽다. (형용사 + as + 주어 + 동사)

97. 당신이 모임에 참석해야 하는 것은 필요하다. (necessary)

98. 만약 내가 날개가 있다면, 당신에게 날아갈 수 있을 텐데. (if)

99. 나는 그가 성공할 것을 확신하고 있다. (be sure of)

100. 창문을 연 상태로 방을 떠나지 마시오. (with + 목적어 + open)

모범답안

1. He seems to be ill.
2. He remained unmarried
3. I keep in good condition.
4. You seemed unable to understand my position.
5. He appears (to be) dissatisfied with the result.
6. The music sounds sweet.
7. They availed themselves of that opportunity.
8. She absented herself from school yesterday.
9. President appointed him minister of foreign.
10. The cold wind turned the leaves red and yellow.

11. We found the room empty.
12. She compelled her son to attend the party.
13. Much money enabled him to study abroad.
14. Please let me know what to do.
15. Did you hear Jack leave the house?
16. She could feel her heart beat.
17. I'm sorry to have kept you waiting.
18. I persuaded her not to go to the party.
19. Don't leave the baby crying.
20. I had my house built by the workers.

21. I couldn't make myself understood in English.
22. I must have [get] my hair cut.
23. No matter where you may go, I will follow you.
24. No matter how hard you may try, you can't pass the test.
25. Be it ever so humble, there is no place like home.
    = However humble it may be, there is no place like home.
26. Whether it is true or not, it is not worth considering.

27. He cannot speak English, let alone French.
28. If I knew her name, I would tell you.
29. If you had left earlier, you could have caught the train.
30. I wish I were rich.

---

31. You should have driven more carefully.
32. He ordered that the boy (should) be sent to the town alone.
33. She proposed that we (should) stay another night.
34. It is natural that he should get angry with you.
35. It is a pity that Tom should lose his wallet.
36. It is strange that you should know so little about it.
37. I took away the water lest the child should drink it.
38. When I was a child, I used to [would] get up early.
39. She is used to singing before large audiences.
40. He talks as if he had been rich.

---

41. It is time that you went to bed.
42. If it were not for your help, I could not do it.
43. If it had not been for his advice, I should have failed.
44. Take an umbrella with you in case it should (may) rain.
45. I will consent, provided that all the others agree.
46. Should it be fine tomorrow, I will play tennis.
47. It is said that he is rich.
48. I had[got] my purse stolen.
49. The most important thing in life is how to live.
50. Do you know what to say about such a topic?

---

51. It is difficult for Tom to master Korean.
52. It is dangerous for Tom to swim in this river.
53. He seems to have been rich.
    = It seems that he was [has been] rich.
54. I worked hard so that I could pass the exam.
55. I will have him wash the car.
56. I had my car repaired.
57. Thank you for inviting me to the party.
58. I have no objection to his going there.
59. He insisted on my going there.

= He insisted that I should go there.
60. Do you mind my smoking here?
= May I smoke here?

---

61. Instead of going out, she stayed at home.
62. Give me one good reason why you did it.
63. People living in cities are very busy everyday.
64. The bird singing on the tree is a lark.
65. My garden is filled with fallen leaves.
66. The leaves fallen on the ground were cleaned by the old man.
67. Three wounded soldiers were taken to the hospital.
68. He has a lovely daughter called Betty.
69. The old man seemed satisfied.
70. I found her weeping in the room.

---

71. I felt something touching my back.
72. I felt myself watched all the while.
73. I had the workers build the house.
74. He went for a walk, with his dog following him.
75. I fell asleep with the TV turned on.
76. It rained all the time, completely ruining our holiday.
77. He stood there with his head leaning against the wall.
78. He sat on the chair, with his legs crossed.
79. He sat under the tree, with his arms folded (crossed).
80. He stood there with his spectacles on.

---

81. She went out with her room empty.
82. Ten years is a very long time to live abroad.
83. Mathematics is a very interesting subject.
84. The audience were deeply moved.
85. Either John or you are in the wrong.
86. Neither you nor he was wrong.
87. Not only the passengers but also the driver was killed.
88. The number of the students in our class is fifty
89. A number of the students in our class are absent.
90. Rich as she was, she was not contented.

91. The higher we go up, the colder it becomes.
92. The harder we study, the more ignorant we find ourselves.
93. We do not know the value of health until we lose it.
   = It is not until we lose it [health] that we know the value of it [health].
   = Not until we lose it [health] that do we know the value of health [it].
94. Scarcely had he gone out when it began to rain.
95. He prided himself on his wealth
   = He took pride in his wealth.
   = He was proud of his wealth.
96. Young as he is, he is very careful.
97. It is necessary that you should be present at the meeting.
98. If I had wings I could fly to you.
99. I am sure of his succeeding.
   = I am sure that he will succeed.
100. Don't leave the room with the window open.

영작문에 꼭 필요한 COLLOCATION

신경향 종합영작문 클리닉 PART II.

1 영작문에 꼭 필요한 COLLOCATION

영작문을 할 때 단어를 하나씩 암기해서 되는 경우는 완전한 영작이 될 수 없다. 단어와 단어가 결합해서 하나의 의미를 만드는 것을 연어(collocation)라 하는데, 이러한 연어를 잘 활용하여 영작 훈련을 하는 것은 자연스럽고 완전한 영어를 완성하는 방법이다.

1. 칭찬 / 비난

1. offer one's congratulations	축하해 주다
2. warmly congratulate	따뜻한 축하를 보내다
3. thunderous applause	우레와 같은 갈채를 보내다
4. give a outstanding performance	뛰어난 공연을 하다
5. take full credit for	완전한 신뢰를 하다
6. receive a standing ovation	기립 박수 갈채를 받다
7. think the world of	최고로 생각하다
8. speak well of	칭찬하다
9. give ~ a big clap	큰 박수를 보내다

영작연습

① 나는 그에게 성공을 축하하는 말을 했다. (offer one's congratulations)

② 그녀는 팬들의 우레와 같은 박수 갈채를 받으며 무대 위에 등장했다.
(thunderous applause)

③ 사람들이 훌륭한 공연을 하고 있다. (give a outstanding performance)

....

④ 그는 내가 한 일에 완전한 신뢰를 했다. (take full credit for)

....

⑤ 남자가 기립 박수를 받고 있다. (receive a standing ovation)

....

⑥ 그 노부인은 자기 고양이를 몹시 좋아한다. (think the world of)

....

⑦ 모두가 그녀를 아주 좋게 이야기 한다. (speak well of)

....

⑧ 손님에게 박수를 보내야 겠군요. (give ~ a big clap)

....

10.	harsh criticism	신랄한 비난
11.	bitterly criticize	신랄히 비난하다
12.	strongly disapprove	매우 반대하다
13.	have a particular liking for	특별히 좋아하다
14.	have the highest regard for	최고로 배려를 하다
15.	have an intense dislike of	몹시 싫어하다
16.	take pleasure	기쁨을 누리다
17.	take offence	화를 내다
18.	give ~ a warm welcome	따듯이 환영해 주다
19.	give ~ pleasure	기쁨을 주다

⑨ 그의 신작 소설은 신랄한 비평을 받았다. (harsh criticism)

⑩ 그들은 나의 제안에 강력히 반대했다. (strongly disapprove)

⑪ 난 항상 바다를 좋아해 왔다. (have a liking for)

⑫ 당신은 우리의 안전을 최고로 배려해야 합니다. (have the highest regard for)

⑬ 우리는 그들을 따뜻이 환영해 주었다. (give ~ a warm welcome)

⑭ 기쁜 마음으로 다음 연설자를 소개해 드리겠습니다. (give ~ pleasure)

2. 주장 / 부인

1.	make serious allegations	심각한 주장을 하다
2.	openly accuse	공개적으로 고소하다
3.	unfounded claims	근거 없는 주장
4.	wrongly accuse	잘못 고소하다
5.	long-running battle	오래 지속된 싸움
6.	back up one's argument	주장을 뒷받침하다
7.	have a argument with	~와 논쟁을 하다
8.	strongly deny	강하게 부인하다
9.	deny a rumor	소문을 부인하다

10. reject a suggestion 제안을 거절하다
11. contradictory evidence 모순된 증거

영작연습

① 그들은 그가 뇌물을 받았다고 공개적으로 고소했다. (openly accuse)

② 그는 최초로 그 기계를 발명했다고 근거 없는 주장을 했다. (unfounded claims)

③ 암으로 인한 오랜 투병 생활 끝에 조지 해리슨은 금요일 세상을 등졌습니다. (long-running battle)

④ 나는 그의 아내와 논쟁을 하였다. (have a argument with)

⑤ 그는 그런 말을 하지 않았다고 강하게 부인했다. (strongly deny)

⑥ 재판에 제출된 증거들은 서로 모순되었다. (contradictory evidence)

3. 결정 / 선택

1.	make a decision	결정하다
2.	come to a decision	결정에 이르다
3.	have second thoughts	재고하다
4.	a degree of uncertainty	불확실함의 정도
5.	arrive at a decision	결론에 이르다
6.	sound judgement	건전한 판단
7.	make a choice	선택하다
8.	give the chance of	기회를 주다
9.	opportunity of a lifetime	평생 한 번의 기회
10.	take advice	충고를 받아들이다
11.	strongly advise	강력하게 충고하다
12.	tough choice	어려운 선택

영작연습

① 우리는 내일까지 결정해야 한다. (make a decision)

② 앨런이 합병에 대해 재고하고 있다면서요. (have second thoughts)

③ 그는 선택하기 어렵다는 것을 알았다. (make a choice)

④ 그들은 그 시합을 이길 기회를 주었다. (give the chance of)

⑤ 이것은 휴가를 즐길 평생 한 번의 기회이다. (opportunity of a lifetime)

⑥ 나는 그녀의 조언을 받아들이기로 결정했다. (take advice)

⑦ 회사는 몇 가지 어려운 결정을 내려야만 했다. (tough choice)

4. 의견 / 생각

1.	firmly believe	단호하게 믿다
2.	share one's opinion on	의견을 공유하다
3.	a great believer in	대단한 신봉가
4.	have reason to believe	믿을만한 근거가 있다
5.	make assumptions	가정하다
6.	an unshakable belief	흔들리지 않는 (단호한) 믿음
7.	trust one's judgement	판단을 믿다
8.	have doubts about	의심하다
9.	think hard	깊이 생각하다
10.	hold the view / opinion	의견을 갖다

영작연습

① 그는 그녀가 무죄라는 것을 굳게 믿고 있다. (firmly believe)

② 나는 규칙적인 운동의 효과를 단단히 믿고 있다. (a great believer in)

③ 어떻게 해서 그러한 가정에 도달하게 되었나요? (make assumptions)

④ 그건 좀 미심쩍은 생각이 든다. (have a doubt about)

⑤ 나는 그 계획이 잘 안되리라는 견해를 갖고 있다. (hold the view)

5. 동의 / 반대

1.	go along with an idea	의견에 동의하다
2.	see one's point	의견을 이해하다
3.	enter into an argument	논쟁을 시작하다
4.	differences exist	이견이 존재하다
5.	differences have arisen	이견이 존재하다
6.	come to (reach) a compromise	타협에 이르다
7.	settle a dispute	논쟁을 끝내다
8.	entirely agree	전적으로
9.	disagree fundamentally	기본적으로 반대하다
10.	bitter dispute	대단한 분쟁
11.	heated argument	열띤 논쟁
12.	a conflict of opinion	의견의 충돌
13.	controversy exist / rage	논쟁이 존재하다
14.	I approve of	~에 찬성하다
15.	I am in favor of	~에 찬성하다
16.	I completely agree that	전적으로 동의하다
17.	I express my approval for	찬성의 뜻을 표하다
18.	I don't agree with (to)	~에 동의하지 않다
19.	I'm against	~에 반대하다
20.	I am opposed to	~에 반대하다

영작연습

① 약간의 문제가 발생했다. (have arisen)

② 만일 이렇게 된다면 이 회사 역사상 우리 독자적으로 분쟁을 수습할 수 없는 첫 번째 경우가 될 것입니다. (settle a dispute)

③ 내가 전적으로 동의하지는 않지만 그쯤 해두겠다. (entirely agree)

④ 그들은 격렬한 논쟁을 벌이다. (bitter dispute)

⑤ 토론이 점점 열기를 띠면서 큰 말다툼이 벌어졌다. (heated argument)

⑥ 그 문제를 두고 의견 충돌이 일어났다. (a conflict of opinion)

6. 기억 / 이해

1.	short-term memory	단기 기억
2.	have a good memory	좋은 기억을 갖다
3.	give a clue	더 도와 달라고 말하다
4.	completely forgotten	완전히 잊다
5.	vividly remember	생생히 기억하다
6.	the memories came flooding back	옛 기억이 돌아오다
7.	blot out that memory	불쾌한 기억을 피하다
8.	trust my intuition	직관을 믿다
9.	unforgettable experience	잊을 수 없는 경험
10.	have a feeling	어떤 느낌을 갖다

영작연습

① 나는 지나간 일을 잘 잊는다. (short-term memory)

....

② 나는 사람의 얼굴을 잘 기억한다. (have a good memory)

....

③ 실마리를 한 가지 줄까? (give a clue)

....

④ 폭발 후에 그 도시는 완전히 잊혀졌다. (completely forgotten)

....

⑤ 나는 학교에 간 첫날을 생생히 기억한다. (vividly remember)

....

⑥ 그것은 잊을 수 없는 경험이었다. (unforgettable experience)

....

⑦ 나는 이것에 대해 예감이 안 좋아. (have a feeling)

....

7. 원인 / 결과

1. immediate cause	즉각적인 원인
2. reduce (minimize) the impact	영향을 줄이다 / 최소화하다
3. positive / negative effects	긍정적 / 부정적 영향
4. cause an uproar	많은 사람들이 화나서 불평하게 하다
5. suffer the consequences	결과에 대해 시달리다

6. have a huge effect on / have a major impact on   큰 영향을 주다
7. make a bad impression   나쁜 인상을 주다
8. have a lot of influence on   많은 영향을 주다
9. cause a sensation   센세이션을 일으키다

영작연습

① 그 사고의 직접적인 원인은 엔진 고장이었다. (immediate cause)

② 그것이 경기에 이기는데 긍정적 영향을 주었다는 증거가 거의 없습니다. (positive effect)

③ 이러한 발전은 그 지역의 지정학에 주요한 영향을 끼치고 있다. (have a major impact on)

④ 내가 있으면 심사위원들에게 안 좋은 인상을 줄거야. (make a bad impression)

8. 성공 / 실패

1. make a breakthrough   놀라운 성과를 이루다
2. a remarkable achievement   놀라운 업적
3. make good progress   상당한 발전을 이루다
4. gain good marks   좋은 점수를 얻다
5. highly effective   매우 효과적인
6. make useful contributions   유용한 기여를 하다
7. go badly wrong   몹시 잘못 되어가다

8. go out of business	파산하다
9. be doomed to failure	실패할 운명에 있다
10. miss the point	중요한 것을 이해하지 못하다

영작연습

① 3개의 금메달을 획득한다는 것은 대단한 성취이다. (remarkable achievement)

....

② 우리는 지금 잘 나가고 있다. (make good progress)

....

③ Pan Am은 올해 세 번째로 파산한 미국 항공회사입니다. (go out of business)

....

④ 그 기업은 실패할 운명이었다. (be doomed to failure)

....

⑤ 당신은 계속 설명해 주시지만, 나는 계속 핵심을 놓치고 있다. (miss the point)

....

9. 시작 / 끝

1. make a promising start	희망적인 시작을 하다
2. make an early start	일찍 출발하다
3. get off to a good start	좋은 출발을 시작하다
4. bring to an end	끝내다
5. draw to a close	끝내다

영작연습

① 그는 일찍 출발하기로 결심했다. (make an early start)

....

② 날씨가 좋았기 때문에, 우리의 여행은 순조로운 출발을 보였다.
(get off to a good start)

....

③ 숙제를 끝마치기 위해 노력하였다. (bring ~ to an end)

....

④ 회의가 끝나 가고 있었다. (draw to a close)

....

10. 성격 / 행동

1.	good company	좋은 친구
2.	a selfish streak	이기적으로 행동하다
3.	have a vivid imagination	생생한 상상을 하다
4.	lose one's temper	화를 내다
5.	highly intelligent	매우 지적인
6.	razor-sharp mind	매우 냉정한 이성
7.	set high standards	높은 기준을 정하다
8.	make snap decisions	빠른 결정을 하다
9.	keep one's temper	화내지 않다
10.	make a fool out of you	속이려 (놀리려) 하다
11.	play a joke on	농담하다
12.	swallow one's pride	자존심을 꺾다
13.	come to terms with	심리적으로 인정하다

영작연습

① 그는 좋은 동료이다. (good company)

② 상상력이 활발해서 상상을 위해 굳이 여행할 필요가 없습니다.
(have a vivid imagination)

③ 제발 화내지 말아. 너를 위해 좋지 않아. (lose one's temper)

④ 나는 매우 지적인 소녀를 만났었다. (highly intelligent)

⑤ 그들은 일반적으로 조용하고 자신과 다른 사람들에게 높은 기준을 정해 놓는다.
(set high standards)

⑥ 항상 화를 참으려고 노력해라. (keep one's temper)

⑦ 그가 날 놀릴 때 난 화가 난다. (play a joke on)

⑧ 그녀는 자존심을 억누르고 열심히 일했다. (swallow one's pride)

⑨ 사람들은 최근의 닷컴사들의 붕괴 현상에 대한 교훈을 서서히 받아들이고 있습니다.
(come to terms with)

11. 신체 / 외모

1.	round face	둥근 얼굴
2.	chubby cheeks	매력적으로 통통한 뺨
3.	pointed face	뾰족한 얼굴
4.	straight nose	곧바로 생긴 코
5.	oval face	계란 모양의 얼굴
6.	slender waist	날씬한 허리
7.	lovely complexion	사랑스런 얼굴
8.	coarse hair	거친 머리카락
9.	well-built	강하고 매력적인 몸을 가진
10.	broad shoulder	넓은 어깨
11.	go grey	흰머리가 되다
12.	go bald	대머리가 되다
13.	thick hair	두꺼운 머리
14.	bushy eyebrow	매우 두툼한 눈썹
15.	jet-black hair	완전히 검은
16.	dumpy woman	작고 매우 뚱뚱한 여자
17.	portly gentleman	뚱뚱하고 둥글둥글한 중년 남성
18.	dishevelled hair	매우 불결한 머리카락
19.	bear a striking resemblance	매우 비슷한 모습을 갖다
20.	have a striking appearance	매우 멋진 외모를 갖다

영작연습

① 나는 둥근 얼굴을 가지고 있다. (round face)

....

② 나는 나의 남동생의 매력적인 통통한 뺨을 좋아한다. (chubby cheeks)

....

③ 그녀의 얼굴은 뾰족하다. (pointed face)

....

④ 내가 질투 나는 것은 그의 곧은 코이다. (straight nose)

⑤ 사람들은 타원형 얼굴을 좋아한다. (oval face)

⑥ 그녀의 허리는 가늘다. (slender ~ waist)

⑦ 그 여자 연예인은 사랑스런 얼굴을 가지고 있다. (lovely complexion)

⑧ 그녀의 단점은 거친 머리카락이다. (coarse hair)

⑨ 그는 건장했지만, 지금은 아니다. (well-built)

⑩ 그는 넓은 어깨와 억센 팔을 가지고 있었다. (broad shoulder)

⑪ 그녀의 머리가 세고 있다. (go grey)

⑫ 내가 20살 때, 새까만 머리를 가지고 있었다. (jet-black hair)

⑬ 나는 레스토랑에서 매우 작고 뚱뚱한 여자를 보았었다. (dumpy woman)

⑭ 그녀는 매우 멋진 외모를 가지고 있다. (have a striking appearance)

12. 가족

1.	nuclear family	핵가족
2.	extended family	대가족
3.	close relatives	가까운 친척
4.	distant relatives	먼 친척
5.	blood relatives	혈족
6.	trial separation	시험적 별거
7.	get a divorce	이혼하다
8.	bitter divorce	쓰라린 이혼
9.	stable home	안정된 가정
10.	deprived home	궁핍가정
11.	confirmed bachelor	결혼 의지 없는 남자
12.	ex-husband (wife)	전 남편 / 아내
13.	broken home	결손가정
14.	start a family	가정을 이루다
15.	have children	아이를 얻다
16.	expect a baby	아이를 기다리다
17.	have a baby	아이를 낳다
18.	the baby is due	아이가 나올 예정인
19.	single parent	미혼이거나 이혼한 부모
20.	bring up children	아이를 기르다
21.	give (grant) custody	(아이에 대해) 법적 보호권을 주다
22.	provide for one's family	가족을 부양하다
23.	set up home	(자신의 집에서) 독립된 생활을 시작하다

영작연습

① 시골지역에 '핵가족'이란 건 없다. (nuclear family)

② 중국에는 대가족이 많이 있다. (extended family)

....

③ Hill 부인은 아주 친한 친척들 외에는 누구도 집에 들이지 않는다. (close relatives)

....

④ 그녀는 나의 먼 친척이다. (distant relative)

....

⑤ Taylor는 그녀의 남편과 이혼했다. (get a divorce)

....

⑥ 그녀는 자신의 이혼에 매우 고통스러워한다. (bitter/ divorce)

....

⑦ 그녀의 전 남편을 들먹인 것은 진짜 큰 실수였다. (ex-husband)

....

⑧ 그는 결손가정 출신이다. (broken home)

....

⑨ 내가 기억하기로는 짐이랑 결혼해서 가정을 꾸리려 했던 것 같은데. (start a family)

....

⑩ 그들은 아이가 넷이다. (have children)

....

⑪ 그녀는 출산을 앞두고 있다. (expect a baby)

....

⑫ 대부분의 편부모 가정은 이혼 때문에 생깁니다. (single parent)

．．

⑬ 그가 아이들을 키우는 것은 힘겨운 일이다. (bring up children)

．．

13. 관계

1. make friends — 친구를 사귀다
2. strike up a friendship — 우정을 만들기 시작하다
3. form (develop) a friendship — 우정을 만들다 (발전시키다)
4. cement (spoil) a friendship — 우정을 다지다 (망치다)
5. friendship grow — 우정이 더 좋아지다
6. close friends — 가까운 친구들
7. casual acquaintances — 조금 아는 사람
8. have a good relationship — 좋은 관계를 유지하다
9. keep in contact — 관계를 유지하다
10. fall madly in love with — 몹시 사랑에 빠지다
11. love of my life — 내 인생의 사랑
12. make a commitment to each other — 서로에게 마음을 쏟다

영작연습

① 그녀는 친구를 사귀는 재능이 있다. (make friends)

．．

② 쓸쓸하면 밖으로 나가 누군가 마음에 드는 사람하고 친구가 되도록 하세요.
(strike up a friendship)

．．

③ 두 남자가 끈끈한 우정을 쌓아가는 모습을 보는 것이 가슴 훈훈하다.
(form a friendship)

④ 그들 사이에 서서히 긴밀한 우정이 생겼다. (close friendship)

⑤ 친한 사이겠구나. (close friends)

⑥ 그들은 아주 좋은 사업 관계를 맺고 있다.

⑦ 모든 옛날 학교 친구들과 계속 연락을 하기는 힘들다. (keep in contact)

⑧ 그녀는 내 인생의 연인이었다. (love of my life)

14. 감정

1.	blissfully happy	매우 행복해 하다
2.	deeply depressed	몹시 우울해 하다
3.	great sadness	대단한 슬픔
4.	bitterly disappointed	몹시 실망하다
5.	let down badly	매우 실망하다
6.	huge disappointment	커다란 실망
7.	mounting anger	커져가는 분노
8.	emotional involvement	감정적 개입

영작연습

① 나는 너로 인하여 매우 행복하다. (blissfully happy)

② 그는 때로는 자살까지 생각할 정도로 극도의 우울감을 느꼈다. (deeply depressed)

③ 자식이 없다는 것은 그에게 있어서 굉장한 슬픔이었다. (great sadness)

④ 그녀가 우리의 기대를 크게 저버린 것 같군요. (let down badly)

15. 집

1.	short-let	단기간 전세
2.	studio flat	1인 아파트
3.	move into a house	이사하다
4.	suitable accommodation	적절한 수용인원
5.	fully-fitted kitchen	완전 설비를 갖춘 부엌
6.	off-road parking	도로 밖 주차
7.	fully furnished	시설을 모두 갖춘
8.	residential area	주거지역
9.	dream home	최고의 집
10.	spacious living room	공간이 넓은 거실
11.	have a wonderful view of	뛰어난 조망을 갖다
12.	add an extension	확장하다
13.	completely refurbished	완전히 개조하다
14.	affordable housing	구입 가능한 주택
15.	take out a big mortgage	큰 저당을 잡다
16.	house-warming party	집들이
17.	feel homesick	향수병을 느끼다

18.	make oneself at home	편하게 하다
19.	feel at home	편하게 느끼다

영작연습

① 그 당시 나는 Olympia 근처에 있는 원룸에 살고 있었다. (studio flat)

② 우리는 새 집으로 이사했다. (move into a house)

③ 그 레스토랑은 완전 설비를 갖춘 부엌이다. (fully-fitted kitchen)

④ 주택가에서는 음악을 크게 트는 것을 삼가해 주시기 바랍니다. (residential area)

⑤ 컴퓨터는 그녀의 최고의 집을 실제로 보여주었다. (dream home)

⑥ 나는 좀더 넓은 거실이 필요하다. (spacious living room)

⑦ 그 아파트는 새 세입자를 위해 완전히 새 단장을 할 것이다. (completely refurbished)

⑧ 이 도시에서는 값이 맞는 집이 드물다. (affordable housing)

⑨ 해를 거듭할수록 고향 생각이 간절하다. (feel homesick)

⑩ 우리 집에 온 것을 환영해. 편히 쉬어. (make oneself at home)

16. 음식

1. junk food — 영양가가 낮은 음식
2. nourishing meals — 영양가가 많은 음식
3. fresh produce — 신선한 농산물
4. food additives — 식품 첨가제
5. processed foods — 가공식품
6. GM foods — 유전자 조작음식
7. food poisoning — 식중독
8. light meal — 가벼운 식사
9. substantial meal — 많은 식사
10. slap-up meal — 크고 좋은 식사
11. gourmet meal — 고품질 식사
12. have a quick snack — 가볍고 빠르게 먹다
13. refreshing drink — 청량음료
14. home-cooked food — 집에서 만든 음식
15. spoil your appetite — 너의 식욕을 해치다
16. reasonably priced — 적당한 가격을 가진

영작연습

① Richard는 영양가 없는 인스턴트 식품도 먹고, 담배도 피운다. (junk food)

② 그는 항상 영양가 많은 음식을 먹는다. (nourishing meals)

③ 나오셔서 신선한 청과물을 구입하십시오! (fresh produce)

④ 어떤 식품 첨가제는 어린이들을 지나치게 나대게 만들 수 있다.
(food additives / hyperactive)

⑤ 우리가 사는 식품은 대부분이 어떤 식으로든 가공처리가 된 것이다. (process)

⑥ 식중독은 죽음을 초래할 수도 있다. (food poisoning)

⑦ 막간에 가벼운 식사를 하다. (light meal / between acts)

⑧ 나의 가족은 집에서 만든 음식을 먹으며 테이블 주변에 모여 있었다.
(home-cooked food)

⑨ 식전에 군것질을 해서 입맛을 망치지 마라. (spoil your appetite)

⑩ 영국에는 적당한 가격의 숙박 시설이 드물다. (reasonably priced)

17. 영화 / 책

1. review the book(film) — 책 (영화) 을 평가하다
2. have a happy ending — 해피엔딩으로 끝나다
3. highly recommended — 강하게 추천된
4. go on the stage — 배우가 되다
5. special effects — 특수효과
6. give a performance — 공연하다
7. box-office hit — 대단히 성공적인 관객 동원
8. compulsive reading — 반드시 읽어야 하는
9. return your library book — 너의 도서관 책을 반환하다
10. renew my library book — 나의 도서관 책을 기간 연장하다
11. skim through a book — 책을 훑어보다

영작연습

① 우리는 이 달의 새 책에서 선정한 책에 대해 서평을 쓰고 있다. (review / pick)

② 그 영화가 해피엔딩으로 끝마치길 바란다. (have a happy ending)

③ 인천 지사에서 귀하를 적극 추천하시던데요. (highly recommended)

④ 그녀는 배우가 됐고 이제 유명했다. (go on the stage)

⑤ 상당량의 특수 효과 작업도 있습니다. (special effects)

⑥ 사람들이 공연을 하고 있다. (give a performance)

⑦ 그 영화는 크게 히트쳤다. (box-office hit)

18. 음악

1. background music — 배경 음악
2. debut album — 데뷔 앨범
3. catchy tunes — 기억하기 즐겁고 쉬운
4. release the CD — CD를 발매하다
5. big hit — 커다란 히트

영작연습

① 배경 음악은 긴장한 여행객들의 마음을 차분히 가라앉혔다.
 (background music / soothing)

② 그녀의 데뷔 앨범은 커다란 히트였다. (debut album)

③ 무척 외우기 쉬운 선율이군요. (catchy tune)

④ 그들의 새 앨범은 큰 히트를 쳤다. (big hit)

19. 스포츠

1. do (gymnastics / judo / weight lifting / yoga / exercises)
   체조 / 유도 / 역도 / 요가 / 운동하다
2. play (games / golf / tennis / baseball / chess / computer)
   게임 / 골프 / 테니스 / 야구 / 체스 / 컴퓨터하다
3. go (fishing / sailing / bowling / swimming / surfing)
   낚시 / 항해 / 볼링 / 수영 / 서핑하러 가다
4. break the world record   세계 기록을 깨다
5. set a new world record   세계 신기록을 세우다
6. world record holder   세계 기록 보유자
7. enter a competition   경기에 들어가다
8. achieve a personal best   개인적으로 최선을 다하다
9. score a goal   득점하다
10. drop the player   선수를 빼다
11. bring on a substitute   후보 선수를 불러내다
12. take the lead   우세하다

영작연습

① 십 년 만에 세계 기록을 깨다. (break the world record)

② 그녀는 높이뛰기에서 세계 신기록을 세웠다. (set a new world record)

③ 그는 마라톤의 세계 기록 보유자이다. (world record holder)

④ 그는 아들이 결승골을 넣는 것을 보고 전율을 느꼈다. (get a thrill / score a goal)

⑤ 네가 앞장선다면 내가 후원하겠다. (take the lead)

20. 건강

1.	catch a cold	감기에 걸리다
2.	develop diabetes (cancer)	당뇨 (암) 가 발전하다
3.	suffer from asthma	천식으로 고생하다
4.	be diagnose with AIDS (cancer)	에이즈 (암) 로 진단을 받다
5.	take vigorous exercise	힘찬 운동을 하다
6.	balanced diet	균형 잡힌 식단
7.	follow a fitness programme	건강 프로그램을 따르다
8.	keep fit	건강을 유지하다
9.	incurable illness	불치병
10.	trivial (minor) ailments	사소한 병
11.	serious illness	심각한 병
12.	relieve the pain	고통을 덜어주다
13.	heavy cold	심한 감기
14.	prescribe some tablets	(알) 약을 처방하다
15.	slight cold	가벼운 감기

영작연습

① 창문을 닫아 주세요. 아니면 우리들 모두 감기에 걸리고 맙니다. (catch cold)

② 어떻게 해서 피부에 암이 생기는지는 밝혀지지 않았습니다. (develop cancer)

③ 균형 잡힌 식사를 하는 것이 중요하다. (balanced diet)

④ 나는 내 건강을 위해 건강 프로그램을 따라했다. (follow a fitness programme)

⑤ 이것이 나의 건강법이다. (keep fit)

⑥ 그녀가 불치병이 있다는 것을 몰랐다. (incurable illness)

⑦ 사소한 질병의 치료. (minor ailments)

⑧ 그는 중병에 시달렸다. (serious illness)

⑨ 의사는 그에게 통증을 덜어주려고 약을 주었다. (relieve the pain)

⑩ 심한 감기를 앓다. (heavy cold)

21. 컴퓨터

1. go online — 온라인에 접속하다
2. connect to the Internet — 인터넷에 접속하다
3. send e-mail — 이메일을 보내다
4. browse the web — 인터넷 검색하다
5. search engine — 검색 엔진

6.	enter the web address	웹 주소에 들어가다
7.	access my company's web-site	나의 회사의 웹사이트에 들어가다
8.	reply to this e-mail	이 이메일에 응답하다
9.	compose your message	너의 메시지를 만들어라
10.	forward the message	메시지를 이동시키다
11.	send an attachment	첨부를 보내다
12.	attach the file	파일을 첨부하다
13.	print out your homework	숙제를 프린트하다
14.	download this picture	이 그림을 다운로드하다
15.	save it to a disk	그 것을 디스크에 저장하다
16.	visit a chat room	채팅방에 들어가다
17.	receive a lot of spam	많은 스팸을 받다
18.	hacking into other people's computers	다른 사람들의 컴퓨터에 해킹하다
19.	re-installing your programs	너의 프로그램을 재설치하다
20.	online shopping	온라인 쇼핑
21.	the computers seem to be down	컴퓨터가 고장난 것 같다
22.	burning a CD	CD를 굽다
23.	back up your work	너의 일 (작품) 을 백업하다
24.	delete a file	파일을 제거하다
25.	hold records on computer	컴퓨터에 기록을 저장하다
26.	display images	이미지를 보여주다
27.	ring tones	전화벨 소리
28.	record video clips	비디오 장면을 저장하다

영작연습

① 기존 연결 방법을 사용하여 인터넷에 연결하십시오. (connect to the Internet)

② 사용자의 이메일 주소는 다른 사람이 사용자에게 이메일 메시지를 보낼 때 사용하는 주소입니다. (send e-mail)

③ 검색 엔진을 이용하는 것조차 짜증나는 수도 있습니다. (search engine)

④ 이 이메일에 응답하다. (reply to)

⑤ 나는 어제 내 숙제를 프린트 해놓았다. (print out my homework)

⑥ 그는 나에게 이 사진을 다운로드해 주었다. (download this picture)

⑦ 이것 좀 디스크에 저장해 주실 수 있으세요? (save it to a disk)

⑧ 그가 채팅방에 들어와 나에게 인사를 했다. (visit a chat room)

⑨ 나는 많은 스팸을 받은 것을 원하지 않는다. (receive a lot of spam)

⑩ 온라인 쇼핑은 별로 믿음이 가지 않아요. (online shopping)

⑪ 나는 그녀를 위해 CD를 굽고 있다. (burning a CD)

⑫ 실수로 중요한 파일을 날렸다. (delete a file)

22. 공부

1.	take an exam	시험보다
2.	conduct a research project	실험프로젝트 실시하다
3.	take a course	수강하다
4.	take a degree	학위를 받다
5.	give a lecture	강의하다
6.	obtain a diploma	수료증을 받다
7.	be awarded a diploma	수료증을 부여받다
8.	receive a A-grade	A학점을 받다
9.	obtain a qualification	자격을 얻다
10.	receive a basic education	기초 교육을 받다
11.	attend the lectures	강의를 듣다
12.	complete the course	과정을 수료하다
13.	hand in your essays	에세이를 제출하다
14.	submit your application	응시원서를 제출하다
15.	leave the course	과정을 철회하다
16.	withdraw from the course	과정을 철회하다
17.	first draft	첫 번째 원고
18.	give feedback	검토해 주다
19.	higher education	고등교육

영작연습

① 나는 내일 역사 시험을 쳐야 한다. (take an exam)

....

② 현재 전 직원은 공장 안전 교육을 받아야 한다. (take a course)

....

③ 나는 마침내 예일 대학교에서 영문학 석사 학위를 받았다. (take a degree)

....

④ 이번 학기에 A학점을 받았다. (receive a A-grade)

⑤ 그들은 시리즈 강의를 듣고 싶었지만, 직장에서 짬을 낼 수가 없었다.
   (attend the lecture)

⑥ 영어 속기와 컴퓨터 사용은 물론 모든 비서 과정을 이수했습니다. (complete ~ course)

⑦ 어제 에세이 제출했니? (hand in your essay)

⑧ 초안이 언제나 마무리 되겠어요? (first draft)

⑨ 그는 고등 교육의 필요성을 느꼈다. (higher education)

23. 일

1. a demanding job	무리한 일
2. apply for a job	일자리에 응시하다
3. steady job	꾸준한 일
4. permanent job	영구적인 일
5. high-powered job	중요한 일
6. carry out work	일을 수행하다
7. complete work	일을 완수하다
8. supervise work	일을 감독하다

9.	take on work	일을 착수하다
10.	have experience in	경험을 갖다
11.	good team player	훌륭한 팀 플레이어
12.	stimulating working environment	근무 환경을 촉진하다
13.	job satisfaction	직업 만족
14.	generous benefits	다양한 혜택
15.	take charge of	책임지다 / 떠맡다
16.	make appointments	약속하다
17.	make the reservations	예약하다
18.	give a presentation	발표하다
19.	make photocopies	복사하다
20.	take early retirement	조기 퇴직하다
21.	arrange meetings	회의 준비하다

영작연습

① 우리는 무리한 일의 걱정거리들에 짓눌렸다. (weigh down / a demanding job)

② 직장에 응모할 때는 인터뷰에 시간을 엄수해야 한다. (apply for a job / on time)

③ 그녀는 고정된 직업이 있다. (steady job)

④ 대학 졸업 후의 인턴쉽이 언제나 풀타임 정규직으로 전환되는 것은 아니다.
(postgraduate internship / permanent job)

⑤ 우리는 필요한 일을 수행할 것이다. (carry out work)

⑥ 언제 그 건축 작업이 완성됩니까? (complete ~ work)

⑦ 나는 영어를 가르친 경험이 있다. (have experience in)

⑧ 직업에 대한 만족도를 월급에 의해서 생각하는 사람도 있다. (job satisfaction)

⑨ 많은 복지혜택은 모든 사원들의 소망이다. (generous benefits)

⑩ 내가 미국에 가 있는 동안 클럽 책임자로 그를 임명했다. (take charge of)

⑪ 다음번 검진 날짜를 정할까요? (make an appointment)

⑫ 예약하셨습니까? (make the reservations)

⑬ 그들은 곧 프레젠테이션을 할 것이다. (give a presentation)

⑭ 그녀는 복사를 하고 있다. (make photocopies)

⑮ 내 비서가 당신께 전화를 해서 모임을 정할 것입니다. (arrange a meeting)

24. 비즈니스

1. go into business — 사업을 시작하다
2. set up a small business — 작은 회사를 세우다
3. small businesses were going under — 작은 회사들이 재정적으로 어려움을 겪다
4. go into partnership — 파트너 관계를 시작하다
5. make a profit — 이익을 내다
6. our business would fold — 우리 회사가 문닫다
7. win a contract — 계약을 하다
8. stiff competition — 힘든 경쟁
9. sales figures — 판매 수치
10. launching a new product — 새 제품을 판매개시 하다
11. customer service — 고객 서비스
12. after-sales service — 애프터서비스
13. running a successful business — 성공적 기업을 운영하다
14. go out of business — 파산하다
15. brisk business — 활발한 비즈니스
16. strike a deal — 거래하다
17. put in a bid — 입찰에 부치다

영작연습

① 그는 내게 실업계로 들어가라고 거듭 권유했다. (go into business)

② 우리는 파트너 관계를 시작할 수 있습니다. (go into partnership)

③ 당신은 그 거래에서 이익을 보았습니까? (make a profit)

④ 그 두 회사는 주요한 계약을 따내기 위해서 협력했다. (win a contract)

⑤ 그 회사는 경쟁사와의 힘든 경쟁에 직면할 것이다. (stiff competition)

⑥ 이번 달 톰슨의 판매 실적이 어떤지 알아? (sales figures)

⑦ 우리는 고객 서비스에 아주 철저하다. (commit to / customer service)

⑧ 우리는 훌륭한 애프터서비스를 제공합니다. (after-sales service)

⑨ Pan AM은 올해 세 번째로 도산한 미국 항공회사입니다. (go out of business)

⑩ 크리스마스 전에는 항상 장사가 잘 된다. (brisk ~ business)

25. 법 / 처벌

1.	obey / observe law	법을 준수하다
2.	enforce law	법을 시행하다
3.	act within law	법 안에서 행동하다
4.	pass law	법을 통과시키다
5.	break law	법을 어기다
6.	law forbids / prohibits	법이 금지하다
7.	rules permit / allow	규칙이 허용하다
8.	rules / regulations apply to	규칙 (규정)이 적용되다
9.	follow the rules	규칙을 따르다

10. regulations require that	규정이 ~을 요구하다
11. comply with the regulations	규정에 부합하다
12. carry out an investigation	조사를 하다
13. go on trial	재판에 회부되다
14. reach a verdict	판결에 이르다
15. fair trial	공정한 재판
16. be severely punished	심하게 처벌되다
17. face a heavy fine	무거운 벌금에 직면하다
18. face the death penalty	사형에 직면하다
19. give a harsh penalty	혹독한 처벌을 하다
20. hard legal battle	힘든 법정 투쟁
21. win a case	승소하다

영작연습

① 여러분은 법률에 따라야만 한다. (obey law)

② 그녀는 법도를 집행하는 직업을 구하고 있다. (enforce law)

③ 그들은 그 법률을 통과시키는 데 동의했다. (pass law)

④ 나는 법을 어겨 자신의 손을 더럽히는 짓은 하지 않을 작정이다. (break law)

⑤ 법률이 이 땅 위에 집을 짓는 것을 금하고 있다. (law forbids)

⑥ 새 규정에 따르면, 중국은행들은 위안화로 저금된 돈을 외국 통화로 바꿔 해외에 투자할 수 있도록 허용됩니다. (rules allow)

⑦ 그 규칙들이 이런 경우에 적용됩니까? (rules apply to)

⑧ Bill을 규칙에 따르게 할 수는 없소. (follow the rules)

⑨ 규정에 따르면 모든 여객 열차는 마을을 통과할 때 서행해야 된다.
 (regulations require that)

⑩ 판사는 재판이 공정하지 못했다는 주장에 화를 냈다. (fair trial)

⑪ 그들은 자신들이 저지른 극악무도한 범죄에 대해 혹독하게 처벌을 받아야 한다.
 (be severely punished)

26. 범죄

1. commit serious offences	심한 위반을 저지르다
2. convicted criminal	죄를 지은 죄수
3. criminal record	범죄기록
4. break into a house	집에 침입하다
5. crime rate	범죄율
6. juvenile crime	청소년 범죄
7. petty crime	가벼운 범죄
8. vehicle theft	차량 절도
9. drug abuse	마약 남용

영작연습

① 기결수는 선거에서 투표가 금지된다. (convicted criminals)

② 그에게는 전과가 있다. (criminal record)

③ 강도가 집에 침입해 물건을 훔치고 있다. (break into a house)

④ 높은 범죄율은 실업에 근거하고 있다. (crime rate)

⑤ 청소년 범죄가 무서운 속도로 증가하고 있다. (juvenile crime)

⑥ 그 나라는 마약 남용이라는 악을 없애야 한다. (drug abuse)

27. 뉴스

1. hit the headline — 헤드라인으로 터지다
2. make headlines — 헤드라인이 되다
3. front-page headline — 1면 헤드라인

영작연습

① 그 사건은 현지 신문들에 대서특필되었다. (hit the headline)

② Jackson의 사생활은 계속 세상을 떠들썩하게 만들었습니다. (make headlines)

28. 돈

1. spend money — 돈을 쓰다
2. save money — 돈을 저축하다
3. waste / squander money — 돈을 낭비하다 / 탕진하다
4. donate money — 돈을 기부하다
5. price is high/low — 가격이 높다 / 낮다
6. rock-bottom price — 아주 저렴한 가격
7. money is tight — 돈이 부족한
8. make a withdrawal — 돈을 인출하다
9. make a fortune — 많은 돈을 벌다
10. money is tied up — 돈이 묶여 있다

영작연습

① 정부는 매년 얼마만큼의 돈을 쓰는가? (spend ~ money)

② 그녀는 인색해지지 않으면서 돈을 저축해 보려고 애썼다. (save money)

③ 돈을 낭비하지 말라. (waste money)

④ 돈을 좀 기부해야 겠어. (donate money)

⑤ 나는 당신이 가격이 높다고 느끼는 걸 이해합니다. (price is high)

⑥ 요즈음 예산이 워낙 빠듯하다. (money is tight)

⑦ 그의 인생의 주된 목표는 재물을 모으는 것이다. (make a fortune)

29. 전쟁 / 평화

1.	war breaks out	전쟁이 발발하다
2.	join the army	군대에 들어가다
3.	fierce fighting	격한 전쟁
4.	all-out war	전면전
5.	open fire	포문을 열다
6.	battle rage	전쟁이 맹렬히 전개되다
7.	peace keeping forces	평화유지군
8.	bring about peace	평화가 오다
9.	negotiate a peace agreement	평화협정을 협상하다
10.	sign a treaty	조약에 서명하다

영작연습

① 1939년에 전쟁이 일어났다. (war breaks out)

② 어린 나이에 그는 입대했다. (join the army)

③ 격렬한 싸움이 계속되었다. (fierce fighting)

④ 기자들이 내게 질문을 퍼붓기 시작했다. (open fire)

⑤ 전투가 머리 위에서 격렬하게 벌어졌다. (battle rage)

⑥ 영국과 프랑스 정부는 모두 수천 명의 병력을 유엔 평화 유지군에 파병했다. (commit / peace keeping forces)

⑦ 그들은 평화를 이룩하기 위해 모든 노력을 다했다. (bring about peace)

⑧ 항복 조약에 서명하다. (sign a treaty)

30. 환경 / 빈곤 / 세계 문제

1. climate change — 기후 변화
2. rising sea levels — 높아지는 해면
3. greenhouse gases — 온실 가스
4. deplete the ozone layer — 오존층이 고갈되다
5. exhaust fumes — 배출 가스
6. fossil fuels — 화석 연료
7. natural disaster — 자연재해
8. live below the poverty line — 최저생계비 이하 생활을 하다

9.	deprived region	궁핍지역
10.	developing countries	개발도상국
11.	global economy	세계경제
12.	combat / radicate / alleviate poverty	가난을 (물리치다 / 퇴치하다 / 줄이다)
13.	political asylum	정치적 망명
14.	asylum seeker	망명신청자
15.	earthquake hit	지진이 강타하다
16.	death toll	사망자 수
17.	sexual exploitation	성적 착취
18.	world-wide problem	세계적인 문제
19.	child labour	어린이 노동

영작연습

① 섬나라들이 지구의 급격한 기후 변화로 인한 피해를 입을 위험도가 가장 높습니다. (climate change)

....

② 온실 가스 배출을 줄이다. (greenhouse gases)

....

③ 자동차가 배출 가스를 내뿜으며 지나갔다. (trail / exhaust fumes)

....

④ 화석 연료는 고갈될 위험에 있다. (fossil fuels / run out)

....

⑤ 많은 자연재해들로 인한 영향은 적절히 계획을 세우면 최소화될 수도 있다. (natural disaster / minimize)

....

⑥ 새 법의 주요 수혜자는 빈곤선 이하로 살고 있는 사람들이 될 것이다.
(beneficiary / live below the poverty line)

⑦ 우리는 그런 개발도상국들을 도와야 한다. (developing countries)

⑧ 세계 경제에 관한 그 신간 서적이 아주 재미있다. (global economy)

⑨ 한 중국 외교관은 스웨덴에서 정치적 망명을 요구했다. (appeal for / political asylum)

⑩ 그 지진은 25년여 만에 가장 심하게 그 지역을 강타한 것이었다. (earthquake ~ hit)

⑪ 일부 보도들은 사망자 수가 훨씬 많다고 보도하고 있습니다. (death toll)

⑫ 아동 노동이 공장에서 착취되고 있다. (exploit / child labour)

31. 시간

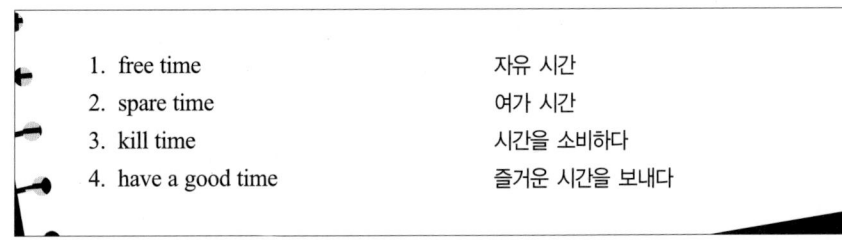

1. free time   자유 시간
2. spare time   여가 시간
3. kill time   시간을 소비하다
4. have a good time   즐거운 시간을 보내다

5. have the time of one's life	생애 최고의 시간을 보내다
6. time goes by (passes)	시간이 지나다
7. small hours	새벽 2~4시

영작연습

① 그의 자유 시간은 나와 일치하지 않았다. (free time / overlap)

② 시간을 허비하지 말라. 일을 하라고! (kill time)

③ 나는 하와이에서 즐겁게 지냈습니다. (have a good time)

④ 아이들은 서커스에서 신나는 시간을 보냈다. (have the time of one's life)

⑤ 세월이 흐를수록 내 기억력이 더 악화되는 것 같다. (time goes by)

32. 소리

1. wind whistles	바람소리가 나다
2. wave crashes	파도가 부딪치다
3. patter of rain	빗방울 부딪침
4. piercing cry	고음의 시끄러운 소리
5. ear-splitting (deafening) sound	귀를 찢는 듯한 (멍하게 하는) 소리

6. muffled sound — 죽인 (틀어막은) 소리
7. roar of the traffic — 차량의 시끄러운 소리

영작연습

① 바람이 문의 갈라진 틈을 윙하고 지나갔다. (wind whistles)

② 나는 지붕에 비가 후드득 떨어지는 소리를 들었다. (patter of rain)

③ 안개 때문에 말발굽 소리가 둔탁하게 들렸다. (muffled sound)

33. 거리 / 크기

1. considerable distance — 상당히 먼 거리
2. within commuting distance — 출퇴근 거리에 있는
3. cover a distance — 어떤 거리를 커버하다
4. fat books — 두꺼운 책
5. slim books — 얇은 책
6. plump (skinny) people — 살 찐 (마른) 사람

영작연습

① 나는 서울의 통근 거리 내에서 산다. (within commuting distance)

② 그 비행기의 항정은 3,000킬로미터이다. (cover a distance)

34. 색깔 / 빛

1. bright colors	밝은 색상
2. color fades	색깔이 바래다
3. pale blue	밝지 않은 푸른색
4. subdued colors	아주 밝지 않은 색상
5. candle flicker	촛불이 깜박이다
6. tinged with gold	금색으로 물들다
7. stars twinkle	별이 반짝이다
8. blacken one's name	명성을 더럽히다
9. shed some light on	빛을 발하다
10. cast a shadow over	그림자를 드리우다
11. under the shadow of	~의 그늘에 가리다

영작연습

① 밝은 색깔과 대담한 필치가 그의 초기 그림들의 특징을 이룬다.
(bright colors / bold stokes)

② 어미 새는 등이 광택 있는 엷은 청색이었다. (lustrous pale blue)

③ 촛불이 잠시 펄럭거리더니 꺼졌다. (candle flicker)

④ 별이 밝게 빛나고 있다. (stars twinkle)

⑤ 오랫동안 사실로 믿어 왔던 것들이 최근의 발견으로 새롭게 조명되었다.
(shed some light on)

⑥ 공주는 기사의 보호 아래 행진하였다. (under the shadow of)

....

35. 촉감

```
1.  greasy hair        기름기 있는 머리카락
2.  dry hair           건조한 머리
3.  oily skin          기름 바른 피부
4.  rough skin         거친 피부
5.  firm pillow        딱딱한 베개
6.  soft pillow        부드러운 베개
7.  tender meat        부드러운 고기
8.  tough steak        거친 고기
9.  blunt pencil       뭉뚝한 연필
10. sharp pencil       날카로운 연필
```

영작연습

① 그의 기름기 있는 머리카락은 마치 한 달 동안 감지 않은 것처럼 보였다. (greasy hair)

....

② 피부를 덜 지성으로 만들려면 그것을 사용하면 된다. (oily ~ skin)

....

③ 내 피부가 이렇게 거친 것이 정말 싫다. (rough skin)

....

④ 연한 고기는 씹기 쉽다. (tender meat)

....

36. 맛 / 냄새

1.	fragrant perfume	냄새 좋은 향기
2.	subtle flavor	미미한 향수
3.	fresh scent	신선한 냄새
4.	bitter coffee	쓴 커피
5.	noxious fumes	유독성 가스
6.	body odor	몸 냄새 (땀 냄새)
7.	give off a smell	냄새를 발산하다
8.	get the flavor of	감을 잡다

영작연습

① 나는 꽃의 향기로운 냄새를 느꼈다. (fragrant perfume)

....

② 블랙커피는 입 안에 쓴맛을 남긴다. (bitter ~ coffee)

....

③ 오븐에서 냄새가 난다. (give off a smell)

....

37. 수 / 횟수

1.	enormous / significant / substantial / considerable number (amount) (엄청난 / 상당한 / 많은 / 상당한) 수 (양)	
2.	tiny number (amount)	수 (양)
3.	odd number	홀수

4. even number 짝수
5. widespread interest (support) 만연된 관심
6. rise sharply (steeply) 급격하게 증가하다
7. fall sharply (steeply) 급격하게 떨어지다
8. increase steadily (gradually) 꾸준히 (천천히) 증가하다
9. remain constant (stable) 지속적으로 (안전하게) 남다

영작연습

① 상당한 수의 동물이 죽었다. (considerable number)

② 2는 짝수이다. (even number)

③ 주택 가격이 급격히 오를 것으로 예상된다. (rise sharply)

④ 가격이 몇 달째 꾸준히 오르고 있다. (increase steadily)

⑤ 그 용기 속의 압력은 계속 변함없다. (remain constant)

38. 동작 / 속도

1. fast train 빠른 기차
2. have a quick glance 빨리 쳐다보다

3.	have a quick shower	빨리 샤워하다
4.	rapid decline	빠른 감소
5.	rapid progress	빠른 증가
6.	speedy recovery	빠른 회복
7.	take swift action	빠른 조치를 취하다
8.	swift response	빠른 응답
9.	prompt payment	신속한 지불
10.	prompt reply	신속한 응답
11.	make a hasty decision	서둘러 결정을 내리다
12.	make a hasty exit	빨리 나가다
13.	top speed	최고 속도
14.	in slow motion	천천히 움직여
15.	slow-moving traffic	천천히 움직이는 차량
16.	have a leisurely breakfast	느긋하게 아침 먹다
17.	gather (pick up speed)	속도를 내다
18.	take a short cut	지름길로 가다
19.	make (take) a detour	우회하다
20.	lose one's balance	균형을 잃다
21.	steer the conversation	대화를 바꾸다

영작연습

① 이 보고서는 라틴 아메리카 지역을 아동 노동에 있어 가장 큰 감소를 보인 지역으로 나타내고 있다. (rapid decline)

② 그들 모두는 아주 제한된 시간 내에 외국어 실력을 빠르게 향상시켜야 한다는 필요성에 공감한다. (rapid progress)

③ 나는 그의 빠른 회복을 빈다. (speedy recovery)

④ 우리는 신속한 지불을 기대하고 있다. (prompt payment)

⑤ 빨리 회신을 보내 주셔서 매우 고맙습니다. (be obliged to / prompt reply)

⑥ 난 성급한 결정을 내리고 싶지 않다. (make a hasty decision)

⑦ 그는 최고 속도로 달아났다. (top speed)

⑧ 다시 돌려서 천천히 움직이는 모습을 봤어. (in slow motion)

⑨ 기차가 속도를 올리기 시작했다. (pick up speed)

⑩ 우리는 범람지역을 둘러서 우회해야 했다. (make a detour)

39. 화법

1. make a speech　　　　연설하다
2. get to the point　　　본론으로 들어가다
3. brief chat　　　　　　짧은 대화
4. have a quick word　　잠시 말하다
5. delicate subject　　　미묘한 주제

6. lengthy discussion	긴 토론
7. speaking off the record	비공개로 이야기하다
8. ask a favor	부탁하다
9. get into conversation	대화로 들어가다
10. join in a conversation	대화에 들어가다
11. make polite conversation	공손한 대화를 하다
12. make an observation	관찰하다
13. strike up a conversation	대화를 시작하다
14. tell a lie	거짓말하다

영작연습

① 그는 연설하기 위해 일어났다. (make a speech)

....

② 요점을 말해 봅시다. (get to the point)

....

③ 잠깐 얘기 좀 할 수 있을까? (have a quick word)

....

④ 부탁을 드려도 될까요? (ask a favor)

....

⑤ 거짓말을 하면 안 된다. (tell a lie)

....

40. 걷는 방법

1. take a stroll — 천천히 걷다
2. go for a walk — 산책하다
3. go jogging — 조깅하다
4. brisk walk — 빠른 걸음
5. gentle walk — 느린 걸음
6. stride confidently — 자신 있게 걷다
7. walking encyclopaedia — 걸어 다니는 백과사전
8. run into problems — 문제에 부딪치다

영작연습

① 나는 산책하고 싶은 생각이 들었다. (inclined / go for a walk)

....

② 이런 날씨에 조깅을 하다니, 그 여자는 정신이 나갔음에 틀림없다. (go jogging)

....

③ 빠른 속도로 걸으면 제 시간에 거기에 도착할 것이다. (brisk ~ walk)

....

④ 문제가 생길 때마다 Jerry는 그의 아버지의 권위에 의존한다. (run into a problem)

....

모범답안

1. 칭찬 / 비난

1. I offered him my congratulations on his success.
2. She appeared on the stage to the thunderous applause of her admirers.
3. The people are giving a outstanding performance.
4. He took full credit for my work.
5. The man is receiving a standing ovation.
6. The old lady thinks the world of her cat.
7. Everyone speaks very well of her.
8. We should give our guest a big clap.
9. His latest novel was subjected to sever harsh criticism.
10. They disapproved strongly of my proposal.
11. I've always had a liking for the sea.
12. You must have the highest regard for our safety.
13. We gave them a warm welcome.
14. It gives me great pleasure to present the next speaker.

2. 주장 / 부인

1. They openly accused the man of taking bribes.
2. He put forward the unfounded claim that he was the first inventor of the machine.
3. George Harrison died Friday after a long-running battle with cancer.
4. I had a argument with his wife.
5. He strongly denied having said so.
6. The evidences given in the trial were contradictory.

3. 결정 / 선택

1. We must make a decision by tomorrow.
2. I hear that Alan's having second thoughts about the merger.
3. He found it hard to make a choice.
4. They've given the chance of winning the match.
5. This is a opportunity of lifetime to enjoy the vacation.
6. I concluded to take her advice.

7. The company had to make some tough choices.

4. 의견 / 생각

1. He firmly believes that she is innocent of the crime.
2. I'm a great believer in taking regular physical exercises.
3. What leads you to make that assumption?
4. I have a doubt about it.
5. I hold the view that the plan cannot work.

5. 동의 / 반대

1. A number of problems have arisen.
2. If this happens, it will be the first time in the history of this company that we have been unable to settle a dispute by ourselves.
3. I don't entirely agree but I'll let it go at that.
4. They have an acrimonious a bitter dispute.
5. The discussion became heated, then a huge argument broke out.
6. A conflict of opinion arose over the matter.

6. 기억 / 이해

1. I have a short-term memory.
2. I have a good memory for faces.
3. Shall I give you a clue?
4. After the eruption, the city was completely forgotten.
5. I vividly remember my first day at school.
6. It was an unforgettable experience.
7. I have a bad feeling about this.

7. 원인 / 결과

1. The immediate cause of the accident was engine failure.
2. There is little evidence that it has a positive effect on winning the game.
3. These developments are having a major impact on the geopolitics of the region.
4. I guess I would make a bad impression on the judges.

8. 성공 / 실패

1. Winning three gold medals is a remarkable achievement.
2. We're making good progress.
3. Pan Am was the third U. S. airline to go out of business this year.
4. The enterprise was doomed to failure.
5. You keep explaining, and I keep missing the point.

9. 시작 / 끝

1. He decided to make an early start.
2. Our trip got off to a flying start because the weather was good.
3. I made efforts to bring my homework to an end.
4. The meeting was drawing to a close.

10. 성격 / 행동

1. He is a good company.
2. I have a vivid imagination so I don't need to travel to imagine things.
3. Please don't lose your temper. It's not good for you.
4. I met a highly intelligent girl.
5. They are generally quiet and they set high standards for themselves and others.
6. Try to keep you temper all the time.
7. I get mad when he plays a joke on me.
8. She swallowed her pride and worked hard.
9. People are coming to terms with the lessons from this dot-com implosion.

11. 신체 / 외모

1. I have round face.
2. I like my brother's chubby cheeks.
3. Her face is so pointed.
4. He has straight nose that's why I jealous him.
5. People like an oval face.
6. Her waist is slender.
7. That actress has lovely complexion.
8. Her weak point is coarse hair.
9. He was well-built, but not right now.
10. He had broad shoulders and powerful arms.
11. Her hair is going grey.
12. When I was 20, I had jet-black hair.
13. I saw a dumpy woman at the restaurant.
14. She has a striking appearance.

12. 가족

1. There's no 'nuclear family' in rural area.
2. There are many extended family in china.
3. Mrs Hill is not at home to anyone except close relatives.
4. She is my distant relative.
5. Taylor got a divorce from her husband.
6. She feels very bitter about her divorce.
7. Mentioning her ex-husband was a real mistake.

8. He comes from a broken home.
9. I remember you couldn't wait to marry Jim and start a family.
10. They have four children.
11. She's expecting a baby.
12. Most single-parent families result when a marriage ends in divorce.
13. It's tough for him to bring up his children.

13. 관계

1. She has a faculty for making friends.
2. If you're lonely, you should go out and try to strike up a friendship with someone you like.
3. It's heartwarming to see two men form a strong friendship.
4. A close friendship gradually grew up between them.
5. You must be close friends.
6. They have a very good business relationship.
7. It's hard to keep in contact with all one's old school friends.
8. She was the love of my life.

14. 감정

1. I'm blissfully happy of you.
2. He felt deeply depressed, even suicidal at times.
3. It was a great sadness to him that he never had children.
4. I'm afraid she let us down badly.

15. 집

1. I lived at that time in a studio flat near to Olympia.
2. We moved into a new house.
3. The restaurant has fully-fitted kitchen.
4. Please refrain from playing loud music in residential areas.
5. The computer gave an illustration of her dream home.
6. I need a more spacious living room.
7. The flat will be completely refurbished for the new tenants.
8. Affordable housing is rare in this city.
9. As years go by, I feel more homesick.
10. Welcome to my home. Make yourself at home.

16. 음식

1. Richard eats junk food and smokes.
2. He always eat nourishing meals.
3. Come out and get your fresh produce!

4. Some food additives can make children hyperactive.
5. Most of the food we buy is processed in some way.
6. Food poisoning can cause death.
7. Eat a light meal between acts.
8. My family gathered around a table eating home-cooked food.
9. Don't spoil your appetite by eating snacks before meals.
10. Reasonably priced accommodation in Britain is scarce.

17. 영화 / 책

1. We're reviewing the pick of this month's new books.
2. I hope the film will end have a happy ending.
3. You are highly recommended from the Incheon office.
4. She went on the stage and was now famous.
5. There is a lot of special effects work.
6. The people are giving a performance.
7. The movie was a huge box-office hit.

18. 음악

1. The background music had a soothing effect on the tense travelers.
2. Her debut album was a big hit.
3. That's a very catchy tune.
4. Their new album made a big hit.

19. 스포츠

1. Break the world record in ten years.
2. She set a new world record for the high jump.
3. He is the world record holder for the marathon.
4. He got a thrill out of watching his son score the winning goal.
5. If you take the lead, I'll back you up.

20. 건강

1. Please close the window, or we'll all catch cold.
2. No one knows what causes the skin to develop cancer.
3. It is important to have a balanced diet.
4. I followed a fitness programme for my healthy.
5. This is what I do to keep fit.
6. I did know that she has incurable illness.
7. The treatment of minor ailments.
8. He suffered from a serious illness.
9. The doctor gave him some drugs to relieve the pain.

10. I have a heavy cold.

21. 컴퓨터

1. Please connect to the Internet using your existing connection method.
2. Your e-mail address is the address other people use to send e-mail messages to you.
3. Even going into a search engine can be nerve-wracking.
4. I reply to this e-mail.
5. I printed out my homework yesterday.
6. He download this picture to me.
7. Can you save it to a disk for me?
8. He visited a chat room, and say hi to me.
9. I don't want to receive a lot of spam.
10. I don't actually trust online shopping.
11. I am burning a CD for her.
12. I've accidentally deleted an important file.

22. 공부

1. I'll take an exam in history tomorrow.
2. All employees are now required to take a course in plant safety.
3. I finally took a degree in English literature from Yale.
4. I receive a A-grade in this semester.
5. Although they wanted to attend the lecture series, they were unable to get the time off work.
6. I completed all the work for the secretarial course.
7. Did you hand in your essay yesterday?
8. When will the first draft be completed?
9. He felt the need of a higher education.

23. 일

1. Weighed down by the cares of a demanding job.
2. When you apply for a job, you should be on time for a job interview.
3. She has a steady job.
4. A postgraduate internship does not always translate into a full-time, permanent job.
5. We will carry out the necessary work.
6. When will the building work be complete?
7. I have experience in teaching English.
8. One may think of job satisfaction in terms of salary.
9. Generous benefits package is all the employees' wishes.

10. I appointed him to take charge of the club while I was in America.
11. Shall we make an appointment for your next checkup?
12. Did you make the reservations?
13. They are about to give a presentation.
14. She is making photocopies.
15. My secretary will phone you to arrange a meeting.

24. 비즈니스

1. He urged me to go into business.
2. We could go into partnership.
3. Did you make a profit out of that deal?
4. The two firms joined forces to win a major contract.
5. The company is likely to face some stiff competition from its competitor.
6. Did you hear about Thompson's sales figures this month?
7. We are totally committed to customer service.
8. We offer an excellent after-sales service.
9. Pan Am was the third U. S. airline to go out of business this year.
10. Business is always brisk before Christmas.

25. 법 / 처벌

1. You must obey the law.
2. She is looking for a career to enforce the law.
3. They agreed to pass the law.
4. I will not dirty my hands by breaking the law.
5. The law forbids building on this land.
6. The new rules will allow China's banks to pool yuan deposits for conversion into foreign currencies and investment overseas.
7. Do the rules apply to a case like this?
8. You can't get Bill to follow the rules.
9. Regulations require that all passenger trains maintain low speed as they pass through towns.
10. The judge reacted angrily to the suggestion that it hadn't been a fair trial.
11. They should be severely punished for the enormity of their crimes.

26. 범죄

1. Convicted criminals are not allowed to vote in elections.
2. He has a criminal record.
3. A burglar breaks into a house and steals things.
4. The high crime rate has its roots in unemployment.
5. Juvenile crime is increasing at a terrific rate.

| | 6. | The country must remove the evils of drug abuse. |

| 27. 뉴스 | 1. | The incident hit the headline in local papers. |
| | 2. | Jackson's personal life continued to make headlines. |

28. 돈	1.	How much money does the government spend annually?
	2.	She tried to save money without being stingy.
	3.	Don't waste your money.
	4.	I'm going to donate some money.
	5.	I understand you feel the price is high.
	6.	Money is so tight these days.
	7.	His main goal in life is to make a fortune.

29. 전쟁 / 평화	1.	War broke out in 1939.
	2.	At an early age, he joined the army.
	3.	Fierce fighting has continued.
	4.	The reporters started opening fire on me.
	5.	The battle raged overhead.
	6.	Both the British and French governments have committed thousands of troops to U.N. peace keeping forces.
	7.	They made every endeavor to bring about peace.
	8.	Sign a treaty of surrender.

30. 환경 / 빈곤 세계 문제	1.	Island countries are most at risk from dramatic global climate change.
	2.	Cut back on emissions of greenhouse gases.
	3.	A car passed by trailing exhaust fumes.
	4.	Fossil fuels are in danger of running out.
	5.	The effects of many natural disasters may be minimized with proper planning.
	6.	The main beneficiaries of the new law will be those living below the poverty line.
	7.	We should help such developing countries.
	8.	That new book about the global economy is very interesting.
	9.	A Chinese diplomat appealed for political asylum in Sweden.
	10.	The earthquake was the strongest to hit the area in more than 25 years.
	11.	Some reports say the death toll is much higher.
	12.	Child labour was exploited in factories.

31. 시간

1. His free time didn't overlap with mine.
2. Stop killing time. Get to work!
3. I had a good time in Hawaii.
4. The children had the time of their lives at the circus.
5. As time goes by, my memory seems to get worse.

32. 소리

1. The wind whistled through a crack in the door.
2. I heard the patter of rain on a roof.
3. The fog muffled the sound of the horse's hooves.

33. 거리 / 크기

1. I live within commuting distance of Seoul.
2. The plane covers a distance of 3,000 kilometers.

34. 색깔 / 빛

1. Bright colors and bold strokes characterize his early paintings.
2. The parent bird was lustrous pale blue above.
3. The candle flickered for a moment and went out.
4. Stars twinkle bright.
5. Recent discoveries have shed new light on some long-held beliefs.
6. The princess paraded under the shadow of knights.

35. 촉감

1. His greasy hair looked like it hadn't been washed for a month.
2. You can use it to make your skin less oily.
3. I really hate having such rough skin.
4. Tender meat is easy to chew.

36. 맛 / 냄새

1. I felt the fragrant perfume of the flowers.
2. Black coffee leaves a bitter taste in the mouth.
3. The oven is giving off a smell.

37. 수 / 횟수

1. Considerable numbers of animals have died.
2. Two is an even number.
3. House prices are expected to rise sharply.
4. Prices have been increasing steadily for months.
5. Pressure in the container remains constant.

38. 동작 / 속도

1. The report finds the most rapid decline in child labor in Latin America.
2. They all share the need to make rapid progress in a foreign language in a very limited time.
3. I wish him a speedy recovery.
4. We expect prompt payment.
5. I am much obliged to you for your prompt reply.
6. I don't want to make a hasty decision.
7. He ran away at top speed.
8. I caught the replay in slow motion.
9. The train began to pick up speed.
10. We had to make a detour round the floods.

39. 화법

1. He rose to make a speech.
2. Let's get to the point.
3. Can I have a quick word with you?
4. May I ask a favor of you?
5. You must not tell a lie.

40. 걷는 방법

1. I felt inclined to go for a walk.
2. She must be insane to go jogging in this weather.
3. If we walk at a brisk pace, we should get there on time.
4. Whenever Jerry runs into a problem, he goes to his father's power.

2 주제별 영작 필수 패턴

1. 제안

- I suggest (propose) that   나는 ~을 제안한다
- My idea is that   내 생각은 ~이다
- What I suggest is that   내가 제안하는 것은 ~이다

ex. What I suggest is that the human way of treating prisoners be found.

2. 사실을 말할 때

사실은
- in fact
- actually
- in reality
- as a matter of fact

ex. In reality, computer games are more popular than ever.

3. ~에 대하여 말할 때

~에 관하여
- with regard to
- regarding
- concerning

이런 점에서
- in this regard
- in this respect

X에 관한 한
- as far as X is concerned

ex. In this regard, music plays a role in treating some illness.
    As far as tennis is concerned, I am a beginner.

4. 예를 들 때

예를 들면
- for example
- for instance
- to illustrate

ex. For instance, the number of attending the conference is increasing.

5. 대조 / 비교할 때

~와 대조적으로	• in contrast to
	• by contrast
이와는 달리	• unlike this
이런 식으로	• in this way
	• similarly
	• in the same way
대조적으로	• on the contrary
	• conversely
~이 반면에	• while (whereas)
~와 비교해 볼 때	• compared with
	• in comparison with
	• comparatively
~에 비례하여	• in proportion to

ex. Some like to play golf, while others like to play tennis.
At night it is cold in the mountain, but in contrast it is hot in the day.

6. 이유를 말할 때

- for this reason — 이런 이유 때문에
- that is mainly because — 저것은 주로 ~ 때문이다
- the basic reason is that — 근본적인 이유는 ~이다
- my experiences have shown that — 나의 경험에 의하면 ~이다
- all things considered — 모든 것을 고려해 보면

ex. For this reason, we can't go there.
My experiences have shown that honesty is the best policy.

Ⅱ. 영작문에 꼭 필요한 COLLOCATION

7. 부연할 때

다시 말해서
- in other words
- to put it another way

- in more technical terms   좀더 기술적으로 말하면
- perhaps it would be more accurate to say that   아마도 ~이 좀더 정확한 말일 것이다.

ex. To put it another way, health is above wealth.
In other words, I fell in love with her.

8. 일반적으로 말할 때

- generally speaking   일반적으로 말해서
- on the whole   대체로

ex. Generally speaking, Koreans likes to eat spicy food.
On the whole, men have a tendency to play soccer.

9. 분류할 때

~로 나누다
- divide into
- classify into
- categorize into
- group into

ex. In general, animals can be classified into 5 categories.
I'd divide the soccer teams into three types.

10. 결과를 말할 때

~의 결과
- as a result of
- as a consequence of

따라서 / 그러므로
- consequently
- accordingly

ex. Accordingly, life-long education must be emphasized.
As a result of winning the election, he became president of the country.

11. 요약할 때

간단히 말해서
- to sum up
- in summary
- briefly
- in short
- it comes down to
- to summarize
- to make a long story short
- in brief
- in a word

ex. In short, soccer is the most popular game in England.

12. 결론을 맺을 때

결론적으로 말해서
- in conclusion
- in the end
- last but not least
- to conclude
- all in all

ex. In the end, we should remove the useless political systems.
Last but not least, you should try your best in conducting the experiment.

13. 강조할 때

- what I want to stress is that   내가 강조하고 싶은 것은 ~이다
- in particular   특히
- above all   무엇보다도
- first and foremost   가장 중요한 것은
- more importantly   좀더 중요한 것은

ex. More importantly, we should eat more vegetables.

14. 대안을 제시할 때

- as an alternative   대안으로서
- alternatively   대신에
- instead of   ~대신

ex. As an alternative, so many people take oriental medicine.

15. 관점을 말할 때

- in that   ~ 점에서
- in consideration of   ~을 고려해 보면
- in view of   ~의 관점에서
- in the light of   ~에 비추어 보면

ex. In the light of my aptitude, I had better do the creative work.

16. 관심을 나타낼 때

- I have a passion for   나는 ~에 대한 흥미가 있다
- I am enthusiastic about   나는 ~에 열정적이다
- I am very keen on   나는 ~에 매우 관심이 있다

ex. I am enthusiastic about playing the piano.

17. 추가할 때

게다가   • in addition   • additionally   • moreover
         • furthermore   • besides

ex. In addition, we should participate in the game.

18. ~함에도 불구하고

- although   • even if
- in spite of the fact that   • nevertheless(nonetheless)

ex. In spite of the fact that I like to go to a concert, I can't play a musical instrument.

19. 목적을 나타낼 때

~할 목적으로   • for the purpose of   • with a view to
               • with the intention of

ex. With a view to learning English, we went to America.

20. 시간 관계

• previously	이전에	• afterwards	나중에
• shortly	곧	• at the same time	동시에
• simultaneously	동시에	• in the mean time	~하는 동안
• meanwhile	~하는 동안	• from then on	그때부터 계속해서
• since then	그때 이래로		

ex. Previously, we used type writers to write a paper.
Simultaneously, we should learn western cultures.

21. 비즈니스 관련 표현

• a counter proposal	반대 제안
• enclose	동봉하다
• We acknowledge acceptance of your order.	우리는 당신의 주문에 대해 받아들이기로 했습니다
• ship	선적하다, 운송하다
• specify	명세서에 기입하다
• It is with deep regret that	~은 매우 유감스러운 일이다
• We can appreciate	우리는 ~에 대해 감사한다
• please do not hesitate to call	주저하지 말고 전화주세요
• unexpected shipment delay	예기치 못한 운송 연기
• a specific shipping date	확실한 선적 날짜
• We appreciate your interest in	우리는 ~에 대한 당신의 관심에 감사드립니다
• We regret to inform you, however, that ~	그러나 우리는 유감스럽게도 ~을 당신에게 알려드리게 되었습니다
• be kept on file	파일에 보관하다
• for future reference	미래용 참고를 위해
• if an opening should arise	빈자리가 생긴다면
• on this newly appointed date	새로 정해진 날짜에
• as of	~현재로
• warehouse	창고
• manufacturing division	생산부
• brochure	소책자
• We would appreciate it if	~해 주신다면 고맙겠습니다.
• This is to inform you that	이것은 당신에게 ~을 알려주기 위함이다
• It is my great pleasure to advise you that	당신에게 ~을 알려주게 되어 매우 기쁘다

- legislature's tariff ruling 입법부의 관세법
- Effective as of June 1, 2009 2009년 6월 1일 현재 발효되는
- be billed 지불되다
- our brand new offices 우리의 새 이름의 사무실들
- estimate 견적서
- transaction 거래
- Our customer has informed us that. 우리의 고객이 우리에게 ~을 알려왔다
- correspondence 서신
- with full payment in advance 완전히 선불로
- letter of credit 신용장
- shipping charges 운송요금
- undersigned 아래에 서명한
- damaged goods 불량품
- non-conforming goods 주문 불일치 물품들
- deduction 공제
- as scheduled 예정대로
- full reimbursement 충분한 변상
- This letter is to remind you that ~ 이 편지는 당신에게 ~을 상기시켜 주는 것이다
- attached invoice 첨부된 송장
- fulfill your obligations 당신의 의무를 이행하다
- A copy of our purchase order 우리의 구매주문 사본
- Unless we receive objection 만약 우리가 반대 의견을 받지 않으면
- within ten days of ~의 10일 이내에
- on the date indicated 명시된 날짜에
- for some time to come 앞으로 다가올 어느 기간 동안
- statements 상세 내역
- the preceding period 이전 기간
- sales personnel 판매사원
- compliments 칭찬 / 찬사
- Congratulations on a job well done. 일이 잘 마친 것을 축하합니다.
- Please accept our heartiest congratulation. 진정으로 축하드립니다.
- Congratulations on the opening of ~의 개관을 축하합니다
- Best wishes for your success 당신의 성공을 기원합니다
- It was with great pleasure that ~은 매우 기쁜 일입니다
- make quite an impression in the industry 업계에서 큰 인상을 만들다
- We provide full service to 우리는 완전한 서비스를 ~에게 제공하고 있다
- make an appointment with ~와 시간 약속을 하다
- at your convenience 당신이 편리한 시간에
- either drop in or make an appointment with. 잠시 방문하거나 ~와 시간 약속을 정하다
- is fully equipped 충분히 갖추고 있다

• We would welcome any questions	우리는 어떤 질문도 환영합니다
• potential distributor	미래의 (잠재적) 공급원
• is compatible with	~와 호환되는
• Our records indicate that	우리의 기록에 의하면 ~을 지적하고 있다
• overdue	기한이 지난
• enclosed envelope	동봉한 봉투
• while this reminder has your full attention	이 독촉장이 당신이 충분한 관심을 갖는 한
• remit your payment	당신의 돈을 송금하시오
• statement of your account	당신 계좌의 명세서
• balance	잔고
• overdue account	기한이 지난 지불금
• enclosed bill	동봉한 청구서
• I am reluctant to	나는 ~을 꺼려 한다
• R.S.V.P (프랑스어) 'reply if you please	(괜찮으면) 답장 주세요
• Yours sincerely	편지의 마지막 인사말 (누군지 정확히 알 때)
• Yours faithfully/ Yours truly	편지의 마지막 인사말 (상대를 잘 모를 때)

22. 변화 관련 표현

• make a adjustment	맞추다
• make a slight alteration	조금 변화시키다
• make a modification	수정하다
• adopt a new approach	새 접근법을 선택하다
• move house	이사하다
• exchange money	돈을 바꾸다
• become available	쓸모 있게 되다
• become successful	성공적으로 되다
• standard of living is improving	생활수준이 향상되다
• problems arise	문제가 생기다

3 영작에 필요한 속담

A

- A bad workman always blames his tools.
  서투른 무당이 장고만 나무란다.
- A bird in the hand is worth two in the bush.
  손 안의 새 한 마리가 덤불 속의 두 마리 보다 낫다.
- A black hen lays a white egg.
  개천에서 용 나다.
- A bunt child dreads the fire.
  자라 보고 놀란 가슴 솥뚜껑 보고 놀란다; 쓰라린 경험은 언제까지나 잊혀지지 않는다.
- Accidents will happen.
  사고란 일어나기 마련이다.
- Actions speak louder than words.
  행동은 말보다 미덥다.
- A drowning man will catch [grasp] at a straw.
  물에 빠진 자는 지푸라기라도 잡는다.
- Adversity makes men, but prosperity makes monsters.
  고생은 사람을 만들고 번영은 괴물을 만든다.
- A fog cannot be dispelled with a fan.
  혼자 힘으로 대세를 막을 수 없다.
- "After you" is good manners.
  양보하는 것이 좋은 예절이다.
- A friend in need is a friend indeed.
  곤경에 빠졌을 때의 친구야말로 진짜 친구이다.
- After a storm comes a calm.
  폭풍이 지난 뒤에 고요가 온다. 비온 뒤에 땅이 굳는다.
- A good appetite is a good sauce.
  시장이 반찬.
- A good beginning makes a good ending.

시작이 좋으면 끝도 좋다.
- A good medicine tastes bitter.

    좋은 약은 입에 쓰다.
- A good neighbor is better than a brother far off.

    이웃사촌
- A hungry ass eats any straw.

    주린 당나귀는 짚을 가리지 않는다. 시장이 반찬이다.
- A journey of a thousand miles begins with a single step.

    천리 길도 한 걸음부터.
- A large fire often comes from a small spark.

    큰 불은 가끔 조그만 불덩이에서 일어난다.
- A leopard cannot change his spots.

    표범은 자기의 반점을 바꿀 수 없다. 세살 버릇 여든 간다.
- A little is better than none.

    조금이라도 있는 것이 없는 것보다는 낫다.
- A little learning is a dangerous thing.

    섣불리 아는 것은 위험한 일이다.
- A little pot is soon hot.

    작은 냄비는 쉬 뜨거워진다; 소인배는 당장 화를 낸다.
- A loaf of bread is better than the song of many birds.

    금강산도 식후경.
- All arts grow out of necessity.

    모든 예술은 필요에서 생긴다.
- All is fair in love and war.

    사랑과 전쟁은 수단을 가리지 않는다.
- All is not gold that glitters. = All that glitters is not gold.

    반짝인다고 다 금은 아니다.
- All is well that ends well.

    끝이 좋은 것은 모두가 좋은 것이다.
- All roads lead to Rome.

    모든 길은 로마로 통한다. 즉, 어떤 목적을 달성하는 데에는 다양한 방법이 있음을 강조하는 말로 모든 일의 궁극적인 귀결은 같다.
- All work and no play makes Jack a dull boy.

    열심히 일하고 열심히 놀아라. = 공부할 때 공부하고 놀 때 놀아라.
- A man is known by the company he keeps.

    사귀는 친구를 보면 그 사람의 됨됨이를 알 수 있다.
- A man is more or less what he looks.

    사람은 대체로 외모대로다.
- A man is not good or bad for one action.

    한 가지 일로 사람의 좋고 나쁨을 판단하지 못한다.

- A man of many talents.
  - 팔방미인
- An Englishman's house is his castle.
  - 영국 사람의 집은 성이다. = 남의 침입을 허용하지 않는다.
- An apple a day keeps the doctor away.
  - 하루에 사과 한 개씩 만 먹으면 의사가 필요 없다.
- An ounce of practice is worth a pound of theory.
  - 말보다도 실천
- An oath and egg are soon broken.
  - 달걀과 맹세는 쉬 깨진다.
- A penny saved is a penny earned.
  - 1전을 절약하면 1전을 번다.
- Appearances are deceptive.
  - 열 길 물 속은 알아도 한 치 사람의 마음 속은 모른다.
- A rolling stone gathers no moss.
  - 우물을 파도 한 우물을 파라!
- Art is long, life is short.
  - 예술은 길고 인생은 짧다.
- As I grew richer, I grew more ambitious.
  - 돈이 많아질수록 더 욕심이 난다.
  - → The more you get, the more you want.
- As one sows, so shall he reap.
  - 자업자득
  - → As a man sows, so shall he reap. 자기가 뿌린 씨는 자기가 거둬들여야 한다.
- As long as there is life, there is hope.
  - 생명이 있는 한 희망이 있다.
- A stitch in time saves nine.
  - 제때의 한 바늘은 아홉 바늘의 수고를 던다.
  - → Prevention is better than cure. 호미로 막을 것을 가래로 막는다.
- As you sow, so you reap.
  - 뿌린 씨는 스스로 거두어야 한다. 인과응보
- A sound mind in a sound body.
  - 건전한 정신은 건전한 신체에 깃든다.
- A tree is known by its fruits.
  - 그 과실을 보면 나무를 알 수 있다; 콩 심은 데 콩 나고, 팥 심은 데 팥 난다.
- Attack is the best defence.
  - 공격이 최선의 방어이다.
- A watched pot never boils.
  - 주전자도 지켜보면 끓지 않는다.

필수속담연습

① 손 안의 새 한 마리가 덤불 속의 두 마리 보다 낫다.

② 행동은 말보다 미덥다.

③ 곤경에 빠졌을 때의 친구야말로 진짜 친구이다.

④ 비온 뒤에 땅이 굳는다.

⑤ 시작이 좋으면 끝도 좋다.

⑥ 좋은 약은 입에 쓰다.

⑦ 조금이라도 있는 것이 없는 것보다는 낫다.

⑧ 작은 냄비는 쉬 뜨거워진다.

⑨ 반짝인다고 다 금은 아니다.

⑩ 끝이 좋은 것은 모두가 좋은 것이다.

⑪ 사귀는 친구를 보면 그 사람의 됨됨이를 알 수 있다.

⑫ 열 길 물 속은 알아도 한 치 사람의 마음 속은 모른다.

⑬ 우물을 파도 한 우물을 파라!

⑭ 자업자득

⑮ 제때의 한 바늘은 아홉 바늘의 수고를 던다.

⑯ 건전한 정신은 건전한 신체에 깃든다.

⑰ 주전자도 지켜보면 끓지 않는다.

B

- Bad news travels fast.
    나쁜 소문은 빨리 퍼진다.
- Barking dogs seldom bite.
    짖는 개는 좀처럼 물지 않는다.
- Beauty is in the eye of the beholder.
    아름다움은 보는 사람의 눈에 있다. = 제 눈에 안경
- Beauty is but [only] skin-deep.
    미모는 거죽 한 꺼풀. 외모로 사람을 평가하지 말라.
- Beggars can't be choosers.
    빌어먹는 놈이 콩밥을 말할까.
- Behind the clouds is the sun still shining.
    고생 끝에 낙
- Better be the head of a dog than the tail of a lion [horse].
    사자 꼬리가 되느니 개의 머리가 되라.
- Better early than late.
    쇠뿔도 단김에 빼랬다.
- Better late than never.
    늦어도 안하는 것보다 낫다.
- Better the last smile than the first laughter.
    최초의 큰 웃음보다는 최후의 미소가 더 낫다.
- Better to be alone than in bad company.
    나쁜 친구와 함께 있느니 보다 혼자 있는 편이 더 낫다.

- Birds of a feather flock together.
  끼리끼리 모인다.
- Birth is much, but breeding is more.
  가문보다 교육이 더 중요하다.
- Bitters do good to the stomach.
  좋은 약은 입에 쓰다.
- Blood is thicker than water.
  피는 물보다 진하다.
- Brevity is the soul of wit.
  간결은 지혜의 정수. = 말은 간결할수록 좋다.
- Business is business.
  장사는 장사. = 인정사정 볼 것 없다.
- By other's faults wise men correct their own.
  현명한 사람은 남의 결점을 보고 자기의 결점을 고친다. = 타산지석

필수속담연습

① 아름다움을 보는 사람의 눈에 있다.

② 빌어먹는 놈이 콩밥을 말할까.

③ 늦어도 안하는 것보다 낫다.

④ 나쁜 친구와 함께 있느니 보다 혼자 있는 편이 더 낫다.

⑤ 끼리끼리 모인다.

C

- Call a spade a spade.
  까놓고 말하다, 솔직히 말하라.
- Cast not your pearls before swine.

돼지에게 진주를 던져 주지 말아라. = 어리석은 자에게 가치 있는 말은 부질없다는 뜻.
- Charity begins at home.
    팔은 안으로 굽는다.
- Coming events cast their shadows before.
    일이 일어나려면 반드시 그 조짐이 있게 마련이다.
- Company in distress makes sorrow less.
    함께 고민하면 슬픔은 덜어진다.
- Constant dripping wears away the stone.
    낙숫물이 돌을 뚫는다.
- Count one's chickens before they are hatched.
    떡 줄 놈은 생각도 않는데 김칫국부터 마신다.
- Curiosity killed the cat.
    호기심이 신세를 망친다.
- Custom is another [a second] nature.
    습관은 제2의 천성이다.
- Cut your coat according to your cloth.
    분수에 맞는 생활을 하여라.

필수속담연습

① 돼지에게 진주를 던져 주지 말아라.

② 낙숫물이 돌을 뚫는다.

③ 떡 줄 놈은 생각도 않는데 김칫국부터 마신다.

④ 분수에 맞는 생활을 하여라.

D

- Danger past, God forgotten.
    뒷간에 갈 적 다르고 올 적 다르다.
- Death is the great leveller.

죽음은 만인을 평등하게 한다.
- Death pays all scores.
  죽으면 모든 셈이 끝난다. 죽음은 온갖 원한을 씻는다.
- Do as you would be done by.
  남이 당신에게 해주기 원하는 대로 남에게 해주어라.
- Do in Rome as the Romans do.
  로마에 가면 로마인의 풍습을 따라라.
- Don't bite off more than you can chew.
  씹을 수 있는 것 보다 더 많이 베어 먹어서는 안 된다. = 과욕은 금물
- Do not go asking for trouble.
  사서 고생을 하지 말라.
- Don't judge of a man by his looks.
  외양으로 사람을 판단하지 말라.
- Do not put the cart before the horse.
  본말을 전도하지 말라.
- Don't make a mountain out of a molehill.
  침소봉대 하지마.
- Drop by drop fills the tub.
  한 방울 한 방울씩 모여 통을 채운다. = 천리 길도 한 걸음부터.
- Do to others as you would have them do to you.
  남에게 대접을 받으려거든 남을 대접하라.

필수속담연습

① 뒷간에 갈 적 다르고 올 적 다르다.

② 남이 당신에게 해주기 원하는 대로 남에게 해주어라.

③ 로마에 가면 로마인의 풍습을 따라라.

④ 씹을 수 있는 것 보다 더 많이 베어 먹어서는 안 된다.

⑤ 외양으로 사람을 판단하지 말라.

⑥ 본말을 전도하지 말라.

⑦ 한 방울 한 방울씩 모여 통을 채운다.

E

- Early to bed and early to rise makes a man healthy, wealthy and wise.
  일찍 자고 일찍 나는 것은 건강, 부, 지혜의 근본이다.
- Easier said than done.
  말하기는 쉽고 실천은 어렵다.
- Easy come, easy go.
  쉽게 얻은 것은 쉽게 없어진다.
- Empty vessels make the most sound.
  빈 그릇은 소리가 크다.
- Even a worm will turn.
  지렁이도 밟으면 꿈틀 한다.
- Even Homer sometimes nods.
  호머 같은 위대한 시인도 때로는 실수를 한다.
  원숭이도 나무에서 떨어질 때가 있다;
  성인도 때로는 실수한다.
- Everybody's business is nobody's business.
  공동 책임은 무책임.
- Every cloud has a silver lining.
  어떤 구름도 뒷면은 밝다.
  = 어떤 나쁜 일이라도 좋은 면이 있다, 괴로움 뒤에는 기쁨이 있다.
- Every dog has his day.
  쥐구멍에도 볕들 날이 있다; 개똥 밭에도 이슬 내릴 날 있다.
- Every Jack has his Jill.
  헌 신도 짝은 있다; 짚신도 제 짝이 있다.
- Every little makes a mickle.
  티끌 모아 태산
- Every man for his own trade.
  사람은 제각기 전문이 있다.
- Every man has his humor.
  사람의 마음은 각양각색
- Everyone has a skeleton in his closet.
  털어서 먼지 안 날 사람 없다.

- Every rose has its thorn.
  모든 장미는 가시가 있다.
- Everything comes to those who wait.
  기다리는 자에게는 모든 것이 성취된다.
- Everything has its time.
  모든 것은 다 때가 있다.
- Everything has a beginning.
  만사에는 시작이 있다.
- Example is better than precept.
  본보기는 교훈보다 낫다; 교훈보다 실례
- Experience keeps a dear school.
  경험이라는 학교는 수업료가 비싸다. = 쓰라린 경험을 통해 현명해진다.

필수속담연습

① 말하기는 쉽고 실천은 어렵다.

② 빈 그릇은 소리가 크다.

③ 호머 같은 위대한 시인도 때로는 실수를 한다.

④ 공동 책임은 무책임.

⑤ 어떤 구름도 뒷면은 밝다.

⑥ 쥐구멍에도 볕들 날이 있다; 개똥 밭에도 이슬 내릴 날 있다.

⑦ 기다리는 자에게는 모든 것이 성취된다.

⑧ 본보기는 교훈보다 낫다.

⑨ 경험이라는 학교는 수업료가 비싸다.

F

- Fine clothes make the man.
  옷이 날개다.
- Fine feathers make fine birds.
  옷이 날개
- First come, first served.
  먼저 온 사람이 먼저 대접 받는다; 선착순 우선
- Fortune favors the brave.
  운명의 여신은 용감한 자의 편이다.
- From saying to doing is a long step.
  말하기는 쉬우나 행하기는 어렵다.

필수속담연습

① 먼저 온 사람이 먼저 대접 받는다.

② 말하기는 쉬우나 행하기는 어렵다.

G

- Gain time, gain life.
  시간을 아끼면 인생을 얻는다.
- Gather roses while you may.
  할 수 있을 때 (젊을 때) 장미꽃을 모아라. = 청춘은 다시 돌아오지 않는다.
- Glory is the fair child of peril.
  호랑이를 잡으려면 호랑이 굴에 들어가야 한다.
- God helps those who help themselves.
  하늘은 스스로 돕는 자를 돕는다.
- Go home and kick the dog.
  종로에서 뺨 맞고 한강에서 눈흘긴다.
- Good luck alternates with misfortune.
  행과 불행은 번갈아 온다.

- Good medicine is bitter in the mouth.
  좋은 약이 입에 쓰다.
- Grasp all, lose all.
  모두 잡으려다 몽땅 놓친다.
- Great barkers are no bites.
  짖는 개는 물지 않는다.

필수속담연습

① 시간을 아끼면 인생을 얻는다.

② 하늘은 스스로 돕는 자를 돕는다.

③ 행과 불행은 번갈아 온다.

④ 짖는 개는 물지 않는다.

H

- Habit [Custom] is (a) second nature.
  습관은 제2의 천성.
- Haste makes waste.
  서두르면 일을 그르친다.
- Hate begets hate.
  증오는 증오를 낳는다.
- Heaven's vengeance is slow but sure.
  천벌은 늦게라도 반드시 온다.
- He catches the wind with a net.
  그물로 바람 잡는다. = 뜬구름 잡는다.
- He who laughs last, laughs best.
  최후에 웃는 자가 승자이다.
- He who hesitate is lost.
  망설이는 자는 모든 것을 잃는다. 쇠뿔도 단김에 빼라.

- He who increases knowledge increases sorrow.
  지식이 늘수록 슬픔도 는다.
- He who would search for pearls must dive below.
  호랑이 굴에 들어가야 호랑이를 잡는다.
- Hindsight is better than foresight.
  선견지명보다는 때늦은 지혜가 낫다.
- Honesty is the best policy.
  정직은 최상의 방책이다.
- Hunger is the best sauce.
  시장이 반찬이다.

필수속담연습

① 습관은 제2의 천성.

② 서두르면 일을 그르친다.

③ 최후에 웃는 자가 승자이다.

④ 망설이는 자는 모든 것을 잃는다.

⑤ 호랑이 굴에 들어가야 호랑이를 잡는다.

⑥ 정직은 최상의 방책이다.

I

- If Jack's in love, he's no judge of Jill's beauty.
  갑돌이가 사랑에 빠지면 갑순이의 아름다움을 판단하지 못한다.
- Ignorance is bliss.
  모르는 것이 약이다; 모르는 동안은 마음이 편하다.

- Ill got, ill spent.
  - 부정하게 번 돈은 오래 가지 못한다.
- Ill news runs apace [fast].
  - 나쁜 소식은 빨리 퍼진다.
- In one ear and out the other.
  - 한 귀로 듣고 한 귀로 흘린다.
- In prosperity think of adversity.
  - 순탄할 때 어려웠을 때를 잊지 말라.
- In unity there is strength.
  - 뭉치면 힘이 생긴다.
- It is a piece of cake.
  - 누워서 떡 먹기.
- It is never too late to mend.
  - 아무리 늦어도 고칠 수 있다; 허물 고치기를 꺼리지 마라.
- It is no use crying over spilt milk.
  - 엎지른 물은 담을 수 없다.
- It is old cow's notion that she never was a calf.
  - 개구리 올챙이 적 모른다.
- It never rains but it pours.
  - 비가 오면 억수로 쏟아진다. = 재난은 반드시 한꺼번에 겹친다.
- It takes two to make a quarrel.
  - 싸움은 혼자서는 못한다.
- It takes two to tango.
  - 두 손뼉이 맞아야 소리가 난다.

필수속담연습

① 부정하게 번 돈은 오래 가지 못한다.

② 순탄할 때 어려웠을 때를 잊지 말라.

③ 아무리 늦어도 고칠 수 있다.

④ 엎지른 물은 담을 수 없다.

⑤ 비가 오면 억수로 쏟아진다.

J

- Jack of all trades is the master of none.
 만물박사는 한 가지도 제대로 못 한다.
- Justice will assert itself.
 정의는 반드시 제대로 돌아온다.

필수속담연습

① 만물박사는 한 가지도 제대로 못 한다.

② 정의는 반드시 제대로 돌아온다.

K

- Kill two birds with one stone.
 일석이조
- Knowledge is power.
 아는 것이 힘이다.

필수속담연습

① 일석이조

② 아는 것이 힘이다.

L

- Laugh and grow fat.
    웃으면 복이 온다.
- Leave a welcome behind you.
    싫어할 정도로 남의 집에 오래 머무르지 말라.
- Leave [Let] well (enough) alone.
    지금 형편이 좋으면 그대로 놔둬라. = 긁어 부스럼 만들지 말라.
    → Let sleeping dogs lie.
- Lend your money and lose your friend.
    돈을 빌려주면 친구를 잃는다. = 돈 거래를 하면 서로 사이가 틀어진다.
- Life is full of ups and downs.
    양지가 음지 되고, 음지가 양지된다.
- Lightning never strikes twice in the same place.
    똑같은 불행을 두 번 겪는 일은 없다.
- Like father, like son.
    부전자전
- Live and let live.
    나도 살고 남도 살게 하라; 공생공존
- Long absent, soon forgotten.
    안 보면 멀어진다.
    → Out of sight, out of mind.
- Look before you leap.
    뛰기 전에 살펴라; 돌다리도 두들겨 가라; 아는 길도 물어가라.
- Look on the bright side.
    좋은 점을 보려고 해라. 긍정적으로 생각해라.
- Love conquers all.
    사랑이 모든 것을 이긴다.
- Love is blind.
    사랑은 맹목적이다.
- Love laughs at a distance.
    반하면 천리 길도 멀지 않다.
- Love levels with all.
    사랑에는 상하계급이 없다.
- Love little and love long.
    애정은 가늘고 길게.

필수속담연습

① 싫어할 정도로 남의 집에 오래 머무르지 말라.

② 돈을 빌려주면 친구를 잃는다.

③ 양지가 음지 되고, 음지가 양지된다.

④ 뛰기 전에 살펴라.

⑤ 좋은 점을 보려고 해라.

M

- Make haste slowly.
  천천히 서둘러라. = 급할수록 신중히.
- Make hay while the sun shines.
  해가 날 때 풀을 말려라. 기회를 놓치지 말라.
- Man does not live by bread alone.
  사람이 빵으로만 살 수는 없다.
- Many dishes make many diseases.
  많이 먹으면 건강에 좋지 않다.
- Many hands make light work.
  백지장도 맞들면 낫다.
- Many a little makes a mickle.
  티끌 모아 태산.
- Marry in haste and repent at leisure.
  서둘러 결혼하고 두고두고 후회한다.
- Marriage is easy, house-keeping is hard.
  결혼은 쉬워도 가정을 지키기는 어렵다.
- Might makes right.
  힘이 있어야 옳게 된다.
- Misery loves company.

동병상련
- Money begets money.
  돈이 돈을 번다.
- Money can't buy happiness.
  돈으로 행복을 살 수는 없다.
- Money isn't the best thing in the world.
  돈이 세상에서 최선의 것은 아니다.
- Money makes the mare (to) go.
  돈이면 안 되는 일이 없다.
- More haste, less speed.
  바쁠수록 돌아가라; 급할수록 천천히 해라
- Much coin, much care.
  돈이 많으면 걱정도 많다.

필수속담연습

① 해가 날 때 풀을 말려라.

② 백지장도 맞들면 낫다.

③ 동병상련

④ 돈으로 행복을 살 수는 없다.

⑤ 돈이 세상에서 최선의 것은 아니다.

⑥ 돈이 많으면 걱정도 많다.

N

- Naked came we into the world and naked shall we depart from it.

빈 손으로 왔다 빈 손으로 간다.
- Nature is the best physician.
    자연은 가장 훌륭한 의사이다.
- Near neighbor is better than a distant cousin.
    이웃사촌
- Necessity is the mother of invention.
    필요는 발명의 어머니; 궁하면 통한다.
- Neck and neck.
    막상막하
    → Diamond cut diamond.
- Never judge by appearance.
    겉 다르고 속 다르다.
- Never put off till tomorrow what may be done today.
    오늘 할 수 있는 일을 내일로 미루지 말라.
- News travels fast.
    발 없는 말이 천 리 간다.
- No gains without pains.
    노력 없이는 이득도 없다.
- No mill, no meal.
    부뚜막에 소금도 넣어야 짜다.
- No news is good news.
    무소식이 희소식.
- None but the brave deserves the fair.
    용감한 자 아니면, 미녀를 얻을 자격이 없다.
- No rule without exception.
    예외 없는 규칙은 없다.
- No smoke without fire.
    아니 땐 굴뚝에 연기 나랴.
- Nothing venture, nothing have [win] [gained].
    모험 없이는 아무 것도 얻지 못 한다; 호랑이 굴에 들어가야 호랑이를 잡는다;
    산에 가야 범을 잡는다.
- No two minds think alike.
    똑같은 생각을 하는 사람은 없다.
- No work, no money.
    일을 해야 돈이 생긴다.
- Nurture passes [is above] nature.
    가문보다 가정교육. 선천성보다 후천성이 더 중요하다.

필수속담연습

① 빈 손으로 왔다 빈 손으로 간다.

② 필요는 발명의 어머니.

③ 겉 다르고 속 다르다.

④ 오늘 할 수 있는 일을 내일로 미루지 말라.

⑤ 노력 없이는 이득도 없다.

⑥ 예외 없는 규칙은 없다.

⑦ 아니 땐 굴뚝에 연기 나랴.

⑧ 모험 없이는 아무 것도 얻지 못 한다.

O

- One man's meat is another man's poison.
    어떤 사람에게는 약이 다른 사람에게는 독이 될 수 있다; 갑의 약은 을의 독.
- One picture is worth a thousand words.
    백문이 불여일견
- One swallow does not make a summer.
    한 마리의 제비로 여름이 오지 않는다; 한 면만으로 전체를 단정하지 마라.
- One hour today is worth two tomorrow.
    오늘의 한 시간은 내일의 두 시간의 가치가 있다.
- Out of the flying pan into the fire.
    갈수록 태산

- Out of the mouth comes evil.
    입이 화근

필수속담연습

① 어떤 사람에게는 약이 다른 사람에게는 독이 될 수 있다.

② 한 마리의 제비로 여름이 오지 않는다.

③ 갈수록 태산

P

- Penny wise and pound foolish.
    한 푼 아끼고 열 냥을 잃는다.
- Pity is akin to love.
    동정은 사랑에 가깝다.
- Poverty brings stupidity.
    가난은 사람을 아둔하게 한다.
- Practice makes perfect.
    연습하면 완전해 진다; 뭐니 뭐니 해도 연습이 제일이다.
- Pride goes before a fall.
    교만한 자 오래 가지 못한다.

필수속담연습

① 한 푼 아끼고 열 냥을 잃는다.

② 연습하면 완전해 진다.

③ 교만한 자 오래 가지 못한다.

S

- Seeing is believing.
  백문이 불여일견
- Slow and steady wins the race.
  느릿느릿 걸어도 황소걸음. 느려도 착실하게 하면 이긴다.
- Small is the seed of every greatness.
  작은 것이 모여 위대함을 이룬다.
- So got, so gone.
  그렇고 그렇게 얻은 것은 그렇고 그렇게 없어진다.
- So many men, so many minds.
  각인각색
- Sour grapes.
  못 먹는 감 찔러나 본다.
- Soon ripe, soon rotten.
  대기만성
- Speak of the devil and he will appear.
  호랑이도 제 말 하면 온다.
- Spare the rod, and spoil the child.
  매를 아끼면 아이들을 망친다.
- Still waters run deep.
  생각이 깊은 사람은 말이 없다. = 잔잔한 물이 깊다.
- Strike while the iron is hot.
  쇠는 뜨거울 때 두드려라.
- Such master, such servant.
  그 주인에 그 머슴.

필수속담연습

① 느릿느릿 걸어도 황소걸음.

....

② 각인각색

....

③ 매를 아끼면 아이들을 망친다.

....

④ 쇠는 뜨거울 때 두드려라.

T

- The early bird will catch the worm.
    일찍 일어나는 새가 벌레를 잡아먹는다.
- The tree is known by its fruit.
    사람은 그 행위로 평가된다.
- There is no accounting for taste.
    제 눈에 안경; 각인각색
- There is no place like home.
    내 집 보다 더 나은 곳은 아무데도 없다.
- There is no royal road to learning.
    학문에 왕도는 없다; 학문에 손쉬운 길은 없다.
- There is no rule but has exceptions.
    예외 없는 규칙은 없다.
- There is no smoke without fire.
    아니 땐 굴뚝에 연기 날까?
- The best fish smell when they are three days old.
    좋은 생선도 사흘이면 냄새 난다. = 귀한 손님도 사흘이면 귀찮다.
- The child is father of the man.
    어린이는 어른의 아버지.
- The darkest hour is that before the dawn.
    동트기 직전이 가장 어둡다. = 최악의 상태는 호전의 일보직전.
- The eagle does not catch flies.
    독수리는 파리를 잡지 않는다. = 매는 굶어도 벼이삭을 쪼지 않는다.
- The end justifies the means.
    목적은 수단을 정당화한다. 모로 가도 서울로만 가면된다; 거짓말도 한 방편.
- The fish always goes bad from head downwards.
    생선은 항상 머리부터 썩는다. = 윗 물이 맑아야 아랫 물이 맑다.
- The grass is greener on the other side of the fence.
    남의 떡이 더 커 보인다.
- The foot of the candle is dark.
    등잔 밑이 어둡다.
- The leopard does not change his spots.

　　　　　세 살 버릇 여든까지 간다.
- The miserable have no other medicine, but only hope.
　　　　　곤경에 빠진 자에게 먹일 약은 희망뿐이다.
- The outsider sees the best[most] of the game.
　　　　　구경꾼이 한 수 더 본다.
- The pen is mightier than the sword.
　　　　　문은 무보다 더 강하다.
- The pot calls the kettle black.
　　　　　똥 묻은 개가 겨 묻은 개를 나무란다.
- The voice of the people is the voce of God.
　　　　　민심이 천심
- Thrift is a good revenue.
　　　　　아끼는 것이 버는 것이다.
- Time flies. = Time and tide waits for no man.
　　　　　세월은 쏜 살 같다.
- To teach a fish how to swim.
　　　　　공자 앞에서 문자 쓴다.
- Too many cooks spoil the broth.
　　　　　사공이 많으면 배가 산으로 간다.
- Truth will prevail.
　　　　　진실은 반드시 이긴다.
- Two of a trade seldom agree.
　　　　　같은 장사끼리는 화합이 잘 안 된다.
- Two heads are better than one.
　　　　　한 사람보다 두 사람의 지혜가 낫다; 백지장도 맞들면 낫다.

필수속담연습

① 일찍 일어나는 새가 벌레를 잡아먹는다.

․․

② 제 눈에 안경.

․․

③ 내 집 보다 더 나은 곳은 아무데도 없다.

․․

④ 학문에 왕도는 없다.

․․

⑤ 예외 없는 규칙은 없다.

⑥ 목적은 수단을 정당화한다.

⑦ 남의 떡이 더 커 보인다.

⑧ 문은 무보다 더 강하다.

⑨ 똥 묻은 개가 겨 묻은 개를 나무란다.

⑩ 세월은 쏜 살 같다.

⑪ 사공이 많으면 배가 산으로 간다.

⑫ 진실은 반드시 이긴다.

V

- Variety is the spice of life.
  다양함이 인생의 묘미다.

필수속담연습   다양함이 인생의 묘미다.

W

- Walls have ears.
  벽에도 귀가 있다. = 낮말은 새가 듣고 밤말은 쥐가 듣는다.
- Waste not, want not.
  낭비가 없으면 부족도 없다.
- What can't be cured must be endured.
  고칠 수 없는 것은 참아야 한다.
- When in Rome, do as the romans do.
  로마에 가면 로마의 풍습을 따르라.
- Where there is a will, there is a way.
  뜻이 있는 곳에 길이 있다.
- Well begun, half done.
  시작이 절반이다.
- What is done cannot be undone.
  이미 끝난 일은 되돌릴 수 없다.
- What is learned in the cradle is carried to the grave.
  요람에서 배운 것 무덤까지; 세 살적 버릇 여든까지.
- When the cat's away, the mice will play.
  호랑이 없는 골에는 토끼가 스승이다.
- Where there is life, there is hope.
  살아 있는 한 희망이 있다.

필수속담연습

① 고칠 수 없는 것은 참아야 한다.

② 로마에 가면 로마의 풍습을 따르라.

③ 뜻이 있는 곳에 길이 있다.

④ 시작이 절반이다.

⑤ 살아 있는 한 희망이 있다.

Y

- You can't tell a book by its cover.
  표지로 책을 알 수 없다. 외모로 판단하지 마라.
- You can lead a horse to water, but you can't make him drink.
  말을 물가로 끌고 갈 수는 있어도 억지로 물을 먹일 수는 없다.

필수속담연습

① 표지로 책을 알 수 없다.

....

② 말을 물가로 끌고 갈 수는 있어도 억지로 물을 먹일 수는 없다.

....

주요 영작문 따라쓰기

신경향 종합영작문 클리닉 PART **III.**

필수구문 50

영작문을 잘하기 위해 알아야 하는 것 중 가장 효과적인 방법 중의 하나가 좋은 문장을 그대로 카피해 보는 것이다. 그러므로 기본적인 문장구조와 어휘에 바탕을 두고 글을 카피해 보는 것이 능숙한 영작문의 지름길이다. 여기서는 에세이를 잘 쓰기 위해 좋은 글을 많이 접해 보고, 이를 토대로 주요 표현과 영작 패턴을 배우기로 한다.

1.	according to ~	~에 따르면
2.	no wonder that ~	~은 당연하다
3.	this is because ~	이것은 ~이기 때문이다
4.	it is reported that ~	보도에 따르면 ~라고 한다
5.	as I pointed out	내가 지적한 대로
6.	the survey shows that ~	조사에 따르면 ~이다
7.	the fact is that ~	사실은 ~이다
8.	it is doubtful whether ~	~인지 의문스럽다
9.	I don't think that ~	나는 ~이 아니라고 생각한다
10.	as far as ~ be concerned	~에 관한한
11.	it's far from ~	~이 아니다
12.	it turns out to be ~	~이라고 판명되다
13.	curiously enough	아주 신기하게도
14.	from a point of view	어떤 관점에서 보면
15.	in the course of time	시간이 지나면서
16.	I have no choice but to ~	어쩔 수 없이 ~하다
17.	in this respect	이런 관점에서
18.	in view of ~	~을 고려하여
19.	on condition that ~	~한 조건으로
20.	personally, I believe that ~	개인적으로 ~라고 믿는다

21.	the point is that ~	요점은 ~이다
22.	there is no doubt that ~	~은 분명하다
23.	I'm very good at ~	나는 ~을 아주 잘 한다
24.	the other side of coin is ~	문제의 또 다른 측면은 ~이다
25.	the 비교급 + 주어 + 동사, the 비교급 + 주어 + 동사	~하면 할수록 더욱 ~하다
26.	I would touch on	내가 간단히 언급하다
27.	it's due to the fact that ~	그 것은 ~때문이다
28.	it's open to question that ~	~은 의문의 여지가 있다
29.	a problem has arisen with ~	~에 문제가 생겼다
30.	as is true of ~	~이 사실이듯이
31.	I think it's high time that ~	나는 바로 ~할 시간이라고 생각한다
32.	whether or not	~이든 아니든
33.	all we have to do is ~	오직 우리가 할 일은 ~ 뿐이다
34.	all that matters is that ~	오로지 중요한 것은 ~이다
35.	as the saying goes	속담에서 말하듯이
36.	irrespective of ~	~에 관계없이
37.	it is needless to say that ~	~은 말할 것도 없다
38.	on the one hand, on the other hand	한편으로는 ~하고 또 한편으로는 ~하다
39.	You must take into consideration that ~	너는 ~을 고려해야 한다
40.	to sum up	요약해 보면
41.	in some detail	어느 정도 자세하게
42.	when it comes to ~	~에 관하여
43.	the reason for~ is ~	~에 대한 이유는 ~이다
44.	the trouble is that ~	문제는 ~이다
45.	I end up ~ ing	내가 결국 ~ 하다
46.	strange as it may sound	이상하게 들리겠지만
47.	for one thing	첫째 이유는
48.	we must consider all the pros and cons of	우리는 모든 찬반을 고려해야 한다
49.	I have the opinion that ~	나는 ~라는 의견이 있다
50.	It seems to me that ~	~인 듯하다

1 주요 구문 따라쓰기(I)

01

It is not only food shortages that the Iraqis will face if the war drags on for months. As fighting keeps raging, there are growing concerns about the health and hygiene of the already dilapidated population due to an acute lack of water and other basic needs. Decades of bad governance and international economic sanctions since the last war in the Gulf have severely destroyed Iraq's infrastructure.

영작가이드

- It is~ that~ : (진주어) ~은 ~이다
- if 주어 + 현재동사, 주어 + 조동사 현재형 (will, can) … : 가정법 현재구문
- food shortage : 식량부족
- as + 주어 + 동사 : ~함에 따라서
- growing concerns : 증가하는 우려
- hygiene : 위생
- decades of : 수십 년의
- sanction : 제재
- drag on : 질질 끌다
- keep raging : 계속 맹위를 떨치다
- due to : ~때문에
- dilapidate : 황폐하게 하다
- governance : 통치
- infrastructure : (사회의) 제반 시설

카피영작문

① 전쟁이 몇 개월을 질질 끌 경우에, 이라크 인들이 직면하게 될 것은 단지 식량 부족만이 아니다.

→ It is not only food shortages that the Iraqis will face (전쟁이 몇 개월을 질질 끌 경우에)

(모범영작) if the war drags on for months

② 걸프에서 지난 전쟁 이래로, 수십 년 간의 잘못된 통치와 국제적 경제 제재는 심하게 이라크의 제반 시설을 파괴시켰다.

→ (수십 년 간의) bad governance and (국제적 경제 제재) since the last war in the Gulf have severely destroyed Iraq's infrastructure

(모범영작) Decades of / international economic sanctions

02

U.N. agencies have appealed for a total of $2.2 billion in emergency funds for the next six months, while the world Food Program alone has asked for $1.3 billion from donor governments to purchase food. **The Korean government would do well to keep up with international efforts to help the war-torn nation by making further donations.**

영작가이드
- a total of : 전체적으로
- do well to : ~하는 편이 더 낫다
- war-torn nation : 전쟁으로 파괴된 국가
- make further donations : 더 많은 기부금을 내다
- emergence funds : 비상기금
- keep up with : 계속 ~하다
- by ~ing : ~함으로써

카피영작문
한국 정부는 더 많은 기부금을 냄으로써, 전쟁으로 파괴된 국가를 돕기 위한 국제적 노력을 계속 하는 것이 더 나을 것이다.

→ The Korean government would do well to (국제적 노력을 계속 하는) to help the (전쟁으로 파괴된 국가) by making 7donations.

(모범영작) keep up with international efforts / war-torn nation

03

Many of them were involved in suspicious real estate dealings or possessed dual nationality, and in some cases they went abroad at the time of child birth and returned immediately after their baby was born.

영작가이드
- be involved in : ~에 관련된
- dual nationality : 이중 국적
- immediately after : ~한 직후에
- real estate dealing : 부동산 거래
- at the time of child birth : 아이 출생시에

카피영작문

그들 중 다수는 의심스런 부동산 거래에 관련되었거나, 이중 국적을 소지했다. 그리고 어떤 경우에는 그들의 아이 출생시에 외국에 가서 그들의 아이가 태어난 직후에 되돌아 왔다.

→ Many of them were involved in suspicious (부동산 거래) or possessed (이중국적), and in some cases they went abroad at the time of child birth and returned immediately after their baby was born.

(모범영작) real estate dealings / dual nationality

04

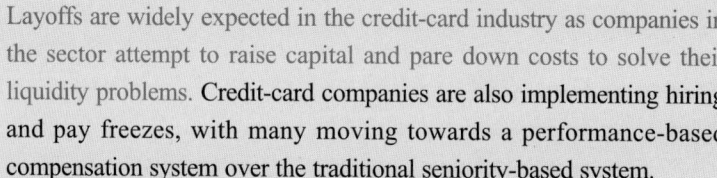

Layoffs are widely expected in the credit-card industry as companies in the sector attempt to raise capital and pare down costs to solve their liquidity problems. Credit-card companies are also implementing hiring and pay freezes, with many moving towards a performance-based compensation system over the traditional seniority-based system.

영작가이드

- layoff : 해고
- pare down costs : 비용을 삭감하다
- liquidity problem : 유동자산 문제
- implement : 실시하다
- hiring and pay freeze : 고용 및 임금동결
- with + 주어 + 분사 (~ing) : (주어) 가 ~하다 (동시상황)
- with many moving towards ~ : 다수가 ~로 향해 움직이다
- performance-based compensation system : 업적 중심의 보상제도
- seniority-based system : 연공서열 중심의 제도

카피영작문

신용카드 회사들은 또한 고용과 임금 동결을 실시하고 있으며, 다수의 회사들은 전통적인 연공서열 중심의 제도에 대하여 업적 중심의 보상제도를 향하여 움직이고 있다.

→ Credit-card companies are also implementing hiring and, (임금동결) with many moving towards a performance-based compensation system over the traditional (연공서열 중심 제도).

(모범영작) pay freezes / seniority-based system

05

In recent months, a few brave directors have decided to turn back the clock and try soft dramas again, perhaps due to fallout from the failure of several high-budget blockbusters last year. **Melodramas typically cost less as they need fewer actors and because most of the scenes are shot indoors, thus making them safer bets for investors.**

영작가이드
- fallout : 악영향
- high-budget blockbuster : 고비용의 대히트작
- typically : 전형적으로
- be shot indoors : 실내에서 촬영되다
- thus making = and thus make bet : 내기, 투자
- investor : 투자가

카피영작문

멜로드라마는 보다 적은 배우를 필요로 하고 대부분의 장면들이 실내에서 촬영되기 때문에, 전형적으로 비용이 적게 든다. 그리고 투자가들에게 그것들을 보다 안전한 투자로 만들어 준다.

→ Melodramas typically cost less as they need (보다 적은 배우) and because most of the scenes are (실내에서 촬영) thus making them safer bets for investors.

(모범영작) fewer actors / shot indoors

06

Furthermore, the popularity of comedy right now has made it more hip for actors and actresses to play funny roles than the traditional somber, dramatic roles, making it all the more difficult for the filmmakers to cast people for melodramas.
For example, up-and-coming film star Kim Ha-neul, who won over male fans with her innocent and quiet image, changed her style entirely for "My Tutor Friend," playing a clumsy college student, and her popularity has skyrocketed.

영작가이드
- up-and-coming film star : 유망한 영화배우
- playing a clumsy college student : 서툰 대학생 역할을 하다

- playing ~ = and played ~ (분사구문의 동시상황)
- skyrocket : 치솟다

카피영작문

예를 들어, 떠오르는 영화배우인 김하늘(Kim Ha-neul)은 그녀의 순진하고 조용한 이미지로 남성 팬들을 얻고 있으며, "My Tutor Friend"를 위해 어색한 대학생 연기를 하며, 전적으로 그녀의 스타일을 바꾸었으며, 그래서 그녀의 인기는 치솟았다.

→ For example, (떠오르는 영화배우) Kim Ha-neul, who won over male fans with her innocent and quiet image, changed her style entirely for "My Tutor Friend," playing a clumsy college student, and (그녀의 인기는 치솟았다)

(모범영작) up-and-coming film star / her popularity has skyrocketed

07

High on the agenda at the two-day consultation are the realignment of 37,000 American troops stationed here and the future of the 50-year-old Seoul-Washington military alliance.

영작가이드

- High on the agenda ~ are the realignment of ~ : 도치 구문
  (High on the agenda ~ 부사구로 문장 앞에 오면 주어와 동사의 어순이 바뀐다.)
- agenda : 회의 의제
- consultation : 회담
- American troops (which are) stationed : 주둔된 미군
- military alliance : 군사동맹

카피영작문

이틀 간의 회담의 의제의 높은 곳에 이곳에 주둔하고 있는 37,000명의 미군의 재배치와 50년된 서울-워싱턴 간의 군사동맹의 미래가 있다.

→ High on the agenda at the two-day consultation are the (이곳에 주둔하고 있는 37,000명의 미군의 재배치) and the future of the 50-year-old Seoul-Washington (군사동맹).

(모범영작) realignment of 37,000 American troops stationed here / military alliance

08

As digital technology advances at breakneck pace, people are exchanging more data files of larger size, such as music, photos and movies, etc. at a faster rate than ever before.
The resulting demand for more storage space, however, can present a host of problems for most corporate and individual users, as most commercially available data-storage devices can often prove to be insufficient or costly to upgrade to keep up with the demand for larger and larger storage capabilities.

영작가이드

- as ~ : 함에 따라
- at breakneck pace : 위험한 속도로
- storage space : 저장 공간
- corporate : 기업
- storage capabilities : 저장 능력
- digital technology : 디지털 기술
- than ever before: 전보다도
- a host of : 수많은
- keep up with : 따라잡다

카피영작문

디지털 기술이 위험한 속도로 발전함에 따라, 사람들은 전보다도 빠른 속도로 음악, 사진, 영화 등과 같은 보다 큰 크기의, 보다 많은 파일을 교환하고 있다.

→ As digital technology advances at breakneck pace, people are (보다 큰 크기의, 보다 많은 파일을 교환하고 있다), such as music, photos and movies, etc. (전보다도 빠른 속도로).

(모범영작) exchanging more data files of larger size/ at a faster rate than ever before

09

Experts and officials predicted Pyongyang will come to the negotiating table with Seoul only after substantial progress is made regarding the North's nuclear issue and the conclusion of the Iraq war.

영작가이드

- negotiating table : 협상 테이블
- substantial progress : 상당한 발전
- nuclear issue : 핵문제
- only after~ : ~ 한 후에 비로소
- regarding : ~에 관한

Ⅲ. 주요 영작문 따라쓰기

카피영작문

전문가들과 관리들은 북한의 핵문제와 이라크 전쟁의 결과에 관한 상당한 진전이 이루어진 후에 비로소, 평양은 서울과의 협상 테이블에 나올 것이라고 예측했다.

→ Experts and officials predicted Pyongyang will (협상 테이블에 나오다) with Seoul only after (상당한 진전이 이루어지다) regarding the North's nuclear issue and the conclusion of the Iraq war.

(모범영작) come to the negotiating table / substantial progress is made

10

Numerous diplomatic efforts have recently been underway to induce the North into a multilateral dialogue on the nuclear issue.

영작가이드
- numerous diplomatic efforts : 수많은 외교적 노력
- be underway : 진행 중이다
- induce A into B : A를 B로 유인하다
- multilateral dialogue : 다자간 회담

카피영작문

수많은 외교적 노력들이 최근에 핵문제에 관해 북한을 다자간 회담에 나오도록 유인하기 위해 진행돼 왔다.

→ Numerous (외교적 노력들) have recently been underway to induce the North into (다자간 회담) on the nuclear issue

(모범영작) diplomatic efforts / a multilateral dialogue

11

Ministry officials explained that apartments have become increasingly favorable to people, as well as being considered as ideal investment vehicles.
Real estate prices last year, in particular, were mostly driven by the skyrocketing prices of apartments.

영작가이드
- investment vehicles : 투자 수단
- real estate : 부동산
- were driven : 움직이다
- skyrocketing : 치솟는

카피영작문

부동산 가격은 작년에 특히 아파트의 치솟는 가격에 의해 대부분 움직였다.

→ (부동산) prices last year, in particular, were mostly driven by the (치솟는) prices of apartments.

(모범영작) Real estate / skyrocketing

12

Most elementary schools do not have enough budget to build safe and fireproof dormitories and operate the team, thus forcing athletes' parents to raise money to pay the coaches and other expenses incurred in training and actual competitions.

영작가이드
- elementary school : 초등학교
- budget : 예산
- fireproof dormitories : 화재 방지용 기숙사
- raise money : 기금을 모으다
- incur : 가져오다
- competition : 경기

카피영작문

대부분의 초등학교들은 안전한 화재 방지용 기숙사를 짓고, 팀을 운용할 만한 충분한 예산이 없으며, 그래서 운동선수 부모로 하여금 코치에 지불할 돈과 훈련과 실제 경기에서 생기는 다른 비용의 돈을 모으도록 강요하고 있다.

→ Most elementary schools do not have (충분한 예산) to build safe and fireproof dormitories and operate the team, thus forcing athletes' parents to (돈을 모으다) to pay the coaches and other expenses incurred in training and actual competitions.

(모범영작) enough budget / raise money

13

> According to the civic activists, the widespread practice is a legacy of Korea's military dictatorship which awarded favors to elite school athletes in their choice of high schools and colleges since the 1970s.

영작가이드
- according to : ~에 따르면
- civic activists : 시민 활동가
- widespread practice : 널리 퍼져 있는 관행
- legacy : 유산, 잔재
- military dictator ship : 군사 독재
- award favors : 혜택을 제공하다

카피영작문

시민 활동가들에 따르면, 1970년대 이래로 고등학교와 대학교를 선택할 때, 엘리트 운동선수들에게 혜택을 부여했던 한국의 군사독재의 유산은 널리 알려진 관행이다.

→ (시민 활동가들에 따르면), the widespread practice is a legacy of Korea's military dictatorship which (혜택을 부여하다) to elite school athletes in their choice of high schools and colleges since the 1970s.

(모범영작) According to the civic activists / awarded favors

14

> Should we hope not to forget the precious lives of the eight boys, we must bring drastic reform to the present elitist physical education at school.

영작가이드
- should 주어 + 동사 = if 주어 + should + 동사 : (주어) 가 ~한다면
- drastic reform : 근본적인 개혁
- elitist physical education : 엘리트주의 체육 교육

카피영작문

만약 우리가 8명 소년의 귀중한 생명을 잊지 않기를 바란다면, 우리는 학교의 현재의 엘리트주의 체육 교육에 근본적 개혁을 가져와야 한다.

→ (만약 우리가 잊지 않기를 바란다면) the precious lives of the eight boys, we must (근본적 개혁을 가져오다) to the present elitist physical education at school.

(모범영작) Should we hope not to forget / bring drastic reform

15

There were no reported casualties in the invading force, but two soldiers and two journalists were killed in a rocket attack south of Baghdad.

영작가이드
- casualty : 사상자
- journalist : 기자
- invading force : 침략군
- rocket attack : 로켓 공격

카피영작문
침략군에 있어서 보고된 사상자는 없었다. 그러나 2명의 병사와 2명의 기자들이 바그다드 남쪽에서 로켓 공격으로 죽었다.

→ (보고된 사상자는 없었다) in the invading force, but two soldiers and two journalists were killed in a rocket attack south of Baghdad.

(모범영작) There were no reported casualties

16

Cabinet-level talks aimed at reconciliation between North Korea and South Korea were canceled Monday after Pyongyang failed to confirm that the meetings would take place, South Korea's Unification Ministry said.
Seoul had hoped to use the meetings to persuade its communist neighbor to scrap its suspected nuclear weapons program. The cancellation is a setback for South Korean efforts to ease tensions between Washington and Pyongyang.

영작가이드

- cabinet-level talks : 각료급 회담
- aim at : 겨냥하다 (목표 등을)
- reconciliation : 화해
- confirm : 확인하다
- Unification Ministry : 통일부
- had hoped to use = hoped to have used : 사용하려고 희망했지만 하지 못했다
- persuade A to B = A가 B 하도록 설득하다
- suspect : 의심하다 nuclear weapon : 핵무기
- cancellation : 취소
- setback : 역전 / 퇴보
- ease tensions : 긴장을 완화하다

카피영작문

북한과 남한 사이에 화해를 목표로 되어 있던 각료급 회담이 취소되었다.

→ Cabinet-level talks (목표를 둔) reconciliation between North Korea and South Korea (취소되었다)

(모범영작) aimed at / were canceled

17

Ten years ago this month, a drunk driver killed my girlfriend. She was only 29. I still miss her and think about her every day. **I think about all the things that intoxicated driver could have done to avoid the tragedy of that night** – things such as calling a cab, letting someone else drive home, or giving the car keys to a designated driver.

영작가이드

- intoxicated driver : 술에 취한 운전자
- could have done : 할 수도 있었을
- designated driver : 지정된 운전자

카피영작문

나는 그 날 저녁의 비극을 피하기 위해, 술에 취한 운전자가 하려고 했다면 피할 수도 있었을 모든 것들에 대해 생각하고 있다.

→ I think about all the things that (술에 취한 운전자) could have done to (비극을 피하다) of that night

(모범영작) intoxicated driver / avoid the tragedy

18

That's when I met Mary. She was Tony's nurse in intensive care. **Mary asked me if Tony was an organ donor.** From the depths of my grief, I was suddenly given a different kind of hope – that other lives could be saved and Tony wouldn't die for nothing. I remember that we had talked about his becoming an organ donor when he renewed his driver's license. **I knew it was what he had wanted.**

영작가이드
- intensive care : 중환자실
- organ donor : 장기 기증자
- from the depth of my grief : 나의 슬픔 깊은 곳으로부터
- renew : 갱신하다

카피영작문

① 메리는 나에게 토니가 장기 기증자였는지에 대해 물었다. (ask ~ if)

(모범영작) Mary asked me if Tony was an organ donor.

② 나는 그것이 그가 원했던 것이었다는 것을 알고 있었다. (what)

(모범영작) I knew it was what he had wanted.

19

At this Iranian border city people don't need to turn on their television sets to watch the latest scenes from the war in neighboring Iraq: They can just look out of their windows. For more than two weeks now the battle raging in southern Iraq around the city of Basra, 30 miles away, has shaken the people of Abadan out of their beds.

영작가이드
- Iranian border : 이란 국경선
- turn on their television set : 그들의 TV수상기를 켜다
- rage : (전쟁이) 한창 벌어지다

카피영작문

이 이란 국경선에서 도시인들은 이웃 이라크의 전쟁으로부터 가장 최신의 모습을 보기

위해 그들의 TV 수상기를 켤 필요가 없다. (turn on)

→ At this Iranian border city people (TV 수상기를 켤 필요가 없다) to watch the latest scenes from the war in neighboring Iraq

(모범영작) don't need to turn on their television sets

20

The American invasion of Iraq is a happy occasion for the country's five million Kurds, mainly because it foreshadows the removal of Saddam Hussein, who committed acts of genocide against them. But it is also welcomed because it has been accompanied by an invasion of foreign journalists.

영작가이드
- occasion : 사건
- foreshdow : 예고하다
- removal : 제거
- commit acts of genocide : 종족 살인 행위를 저지르다

카피영작문

이라크에 대한 미국의 침공은 그 나라의 5백만 Kruds족에게는 행복한 사건이다, 주로 그것은 그들에 대해 종족 살인 행위를 저지른 사담 후세인의 제거를 예고하기 때문이다.

→ (이라크에 대한 미국의 침공) is a happy occasion for the country's five million Kurds, mainly because it foreshadows the removal of Saddam Hussein, who (종족 살인 행위를 저지르다) against them.

(모범영작) The American invasion of Iraq / committed acts of genocide

21

The World Health Organization (WHO) has **issued a global health alert** for authorities to **be aware of** a new atypical pneumonia called Severe Acute Respiratory Syndrome (SARS).

영작가이드

- World Health Organization (WHO) : 세계보건기구
- issue : 만들다, 발생하다
- authority : 정부당국자
- be aware of : ~을 알다
- atypical pneumonia : 비전형적 폐렴
- Severe Acute Respiratory Syndrome : 급성 호흡기 증후군

카피영작문

세계보건기구(WHO)는 세계 당국들이 SARS라는 새로운 비전형적 폐렴을 알도록, 세계 건강 경보를 발효했다. (issue)

→ The World Health Organization (WHO) has (세계 건강 경보를 발효했다) for authorities to (알도록) a new atypical pneumonia called SARS.

(모범영작) issued a global health alert / be aware of

The CMO has been convening a meeting every day with State and Territory health officials and infectious diseases specialists.

영작가이드

- convene a meeting : 회의를 열다
- infectious diseases specialists : 전염병 전문가

카피영작문

최고의료책임자(CMO)는 국가-지역의료 관리들과 전염병 전문가들과 매일 회의를 개최해 오고 있다. (convene)

→ The CMO has been (회의를 개최하다) every day with State and Territory health officials and infectious diseases specialists

(모범영작) convening a meeting

23

The numbers of people under investigation changes rapidly.

영작가이드

• under investigation : 조사 중에 있는

카피영작문

조사 받고 있는 수많은 사람들이 빠르게 변화하고 있다.

→ The numbers of people (조사 받고 있는) changes rapidly

(모범영작) under investigation

2 주요 구문 따라쓰기(II)

01

1. It was celebrated in much the same way as it is today with parties and dancing into the late hours of the night.
2. French children fool their friends by taping a paper fish to their friends' backs.
3. Today Americans play small tricks on friends and strangers alike on the first of April.
4. College students set their clocks an hour behind, so their roommates show up to the wrong class
5. Some practical jokes are kept up the whole day before the victim realizes what day it is.

주요표현

- celebrate : 기념하다
- show up : 나타나다
- play a trick on : 골탕 먹이다
- practical joke : 짓궂은 장난

영작체크

① 그것은 오늘날과 마찬가지로 파티와 춤을 밤늦은 시간까지 하면서 기념된다.
(celebrate / in much the same way / dancing into the late hours of the night)

(모범영작) It was celebrated in much the same way as it is today with parties and dancing into the late hours of the night.

② 프랑스 아이들은 그들의 친구들의 등에 종이 물고기를 테이프로 붙이면서 그들을 골려준다. (fool / tape / back)

(모범영작) French children fool their friends by taping a paper fish to their friends' backs.

③ 오늘날 미국인들은 4월 1일에 친구들이나 이방인들을 똑같이 가볍게 골탕을 먹인다. (play trick on / alike)

(모범영작) Today Americans play small tricks on friends and strangers alike on the first of April.

④ 일부 대학생들이 시계를 한 시간 뒤로 돌려놓아서, 그들의 급우들이 잘못된 수업에 나타나게 된다. (set one's clock ~ behind / show up)

(모범영작) College students set their clocks an hour behind, so their roommates show up to the wrong class

⑤ 몇몇 짓궂은 장난들은, 그 희생자가 그 날이 무슨 날인지를 깨달을 때까지 하루 종일 계속된다.
(practical jokes / keep up / victim)

(모범영작) Some practical jokes are kept up the whole day before the victim realizes what day it is.

02

1. The deadly SARS virus sweeping through China and Southeast Asia is posing an increasingly serious threat to local exporters already struggling with war-related damages.
2. In a related blow to the national economy, an international economic forum slated to be held in Seoul next week was cancelled partly due to growing fears.
3. A paper manufacturer is suffering from a sharp decrease in demand due to reluctance by foreign buyers to make a visit for purchase.
4. Manufacturers of surgical supplies, such as masks, disposable gloves, sterilizing disinfectants and soaps, which are experiencing skyrocketing demands - have been given the full support of the ministry in stepping up overseas sales of their products.

주요표현

- sweeping : 휩쓰는
- posing an increasingly serious threat to : ~에 점차 심각한 위협을 제기하면서
- a growing number of local firms : 늘어나는 숫자의 지역회사들
- outbreak: 돌발
- cancellation : 취소
- spurred by : ~에 의해 촉발된
- comprehensive countermeasures : 포괄적 대응조치들
- withdrew its itinerary : 그 일정을 철회하다
- downgrade : 하향 조정하다
- flurry : 혼란 / 소동
- surgical supplies : 수술장비
- disposable gloves : 1회용 장갑
- sterilizing disinfectants : 소독용 감염 제거제
- in stepping up overseas sales : 해외수출을 증가시킴에 있어
- SARS-free nation : 사스 없는 국가
- skyrocketing demands : 치솟는 수요

영작체크

① 중국과 동남아시아를 휩쓸고 있는 치명적인 사스 바이러스가, 이미 전쟁과 관련된 피해와 싸우고 있는 지역 수출업자들에게 점점 심각한 위협을 제기하고 있다.
(sweep through / pose a threat to / struggle with / war-related)

(모범영작) The deadly SARS virus sweeping through China and Southeast Asia is posing an increasingly serious threat to local exporters already struggling with war-related damages.

② 국가 경제에 대한 관련된 충격 속에서, 다음 주에 서울에서 개최 예정인 국제 포럼(회의)이 부분적으로 증가하는 공포 때문에 취소되었다.
(related blow to / national economy / forum / slate / cancel / due to)

(모범영작) In a related blow to the national economy, an international economic forum slated to be held in Seoul next week was cancelled partly due to growing fears.

③ 어떤 종이 제조업자는, 구입하기 위해 방문하려는 외국 바이어들의 꺼려함 때문에, 급격한 수요의 감소로 시달리고 있다.
(paper manufacturer / suffer from / sharp decrease / due to / purchase)

(모범영작) A paper manufacturer is suffering from a sharp decrease in demand due to reluctance by foreign buyers to make a visit for purchase.

④ 치솟는 수요를 경험하고 있는 마스크, 1회용 장갑, 소독용 감염 제거제와 같은 수술 장비 제조업자들은, 그들의 제품의 해외 수출을 증가시킴에 있어, 국가 담당 부서의 전폭적인 지지를 받아오고 있다.
(surgical supplies / such as / disposable gloves / sterilizing disinfectant / skyrocketing demands / step up / overseas sales)

(모범영작) Manufacturers of surgical supplies, such as masks, disposable gloves, sterilizing disinfectants and soaps, which are experiencing skyrocketing demands - have been given the full support of the ministry in stepping up overseas sales of their products.

03

1. Medical experts have warned that it would just be "a matter of time."
2. More than 2,300 people around the world have been infected 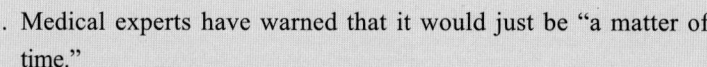 driving the international community into a panic.

주요표현
- epicenter : 진원지
- as of yesterday : 어제 현재
- unprecedented move : 전례 없는 움직임
- inbound : 본국 행의
- global death toll : 세계적 사망자 숫자
- so-called : 소위
- time-honored custom : 유서 깊은 관습
- vigil : 경계 / 감시

영작체크

① 의료 전문가들은 그것은 단지 시간문제가 될 것이라고 경고해 왔다.
(medical experts / a matter of time)

(모범영작) Medical experts have warned that it would just be "a matter of time."

② 전세계적으로 2,300명 이상의 사람들이 국제사회를 공포로 몰아가면서 감염되어 왔다.
(more than / infect / international community / panic)

(모범영작) More than 2,300 people around the world have been infected driving the international community into a panic.

04

1. As yesterday's meeting was the first in a series of negotiations to continue until Autumn, the two sides focused on exchanging opinions on major issues.
2. It is not known whether the U.S. expressed a wish to reduce its number of troops in South Korea during the talks.
3. Results of the negotiations, which will resume next month, will be announced at a press conference to be held jointly by South Korean and U.S. negotiators at the Defense Ministry this afternoon.

주요표현

- bring about : 야기하다
- respectively : 제각기
- headquarters : 본부
- relocation : 재배치
- clustered : 모여 있는
- resume : 재개하다
- Foreign Affairs-Trade Ministry : 통상외교부
- special envoy : 특사
- 50-year-old alliance : 50년의 동맹
- Defense Ministry : 국방부
- focused on : 초점을 맞추다
- reshuffle : 개각
- resume : 재개하다
- press conference : 기자회견
- took part in : 참가했다

영작체크

① 어제의 회담은 8월까지 계속될 일련의 협상 중 첫 번째 것이기 때문에, 두 진영은 주요 문제에 관해 의견을 맞추는 데 초점을 맞추고 있다.
(negotiation / focus on / major issue)

(모범영작) As yesterday's meeting was the first in a series of negotiations to continue until Autumn, the two sides focused on exchanging opinions on major issues.

② 미국이 회담 도중에 남한에 주둔하고 있는 군대의 숫자를 줄이려는 희망을 표현했는

지 여부는 알려지지 않고 있다. (whether / reduce / troop / talks)

(모범영작) It is not known whether the U.S. expressed a wish to reduce its number of troops in South Korea during the talks.

③ 다음 달 재개될 협상 결과는 오늘 오후 국방부에서 남한과 미국 협상단이 공동을 개최하는 기자회견에서 발표될 것이다.
(negotiation / resume / press conference / jointly / Defense Ministry)

(모범영작) Results of the negotiations, which will resume next month, will be announced at a press conference to be held jointly by South Korean and U.S. negotiators at the Defense Ministry this afternoon.

05

1. Many people are nervous about speculative news reports, both local and foreign, that North Korea will be the next target of U.S. strike after the military conflict in Iraq unless Pyongyang gives up its nuclear ambitions.
2. In this regard, North Korea needs to resume talks with the South as soon as possible so as to peacefully put an end to the nuclear crisis on the peninsula through close cooperation.

주요표현

- unreliability : 불신
- was scheduled to : ~할 예정이다
- abort : 폐기하다, 취소하다
- called off : 취소하다
- commemoration ceremony : 기념식
- escalating the tension : 긴장을 높이는
- bilateral dialog : 양자회담
- plunged into : 뛰어 들다
- under any circumstances : 어떤 환경 하에서도
- get suspicious of : ~을 의심하다
- In this regard : 이런 점에서
- ministerial meeting : 장관 회담
- It is speculated that : ~은 추정되다
- impending dispatch : 다가온 파견
- futile : 소용없는
- inauguration : 취임
- speculative : 근거 없는, 추정되는
- multilateral negotiations : 다자간 협상
- military turmoil : 군사 문제
- induced (to) : ~하도록 만들다
- nuclear feud : 핵 불화
- put an end to : ~을 끝내다

영작체크

① 많은 사람들은, 만약 평양측이 핵 야망을 포기하지 않으면, 북한이 이라크 내의 군사 분쟁 후에 미국의 다음 목표가 될 것이라는 국내와 외국의 추측성 뉴스 보도에 대해 초조해 하고 있다. (be nervous about / military conflict)

_____

_____

(모범영작) Many people are nervous about speculative news reports, both local and foreign, that North Korea will be the next target of U.S. strike after the military conflict in Iraq unless Pyongyang gives up its nuclear ambitions.

② 이런 점에서 북한은 친밀한 협력을 통해 (한)반도의 핵 위기를 평화롭게 종식시키기 위해 가능한 빨리 남한과 회담을 재개할 필요가 있다.
(in this regard / resume / put an end to)

_____

_____

(모범영작) In this regard, North Korea needs to resume talks with the South as soon as possible so as to peacefully put an end to the nuclear crisis on the peninsula through close cooperation.

06

1. Like other advanced countries, the nation is now faced with a serious social problem of increasing numbers of old people because of the rising life expectancy and declining birth rate.
2. In connection with improving the welfare and health of aged people, the central government and local autonomous administrations also need to concentrate efforts to expand job opportunities for them.
3. As the government encourages couples to have more babies, birth control, which has been in force since 1960, is discarded apparently in view of the dwindling productive workforce due to the expanding elderly population.

주요표현

- advanced countries : 선진국
- corporate restructuring : 기업 구조조정
- backdrop : 배경
- stroke : 발작
- government subsidies : 정부보조금

- life expectancy : 기대수명
- unprecedented : 전례 없는
- state-run sanatoriums : 국영 요양소
- alzheimer : 치매
- in view of : ~의 관점에서

- dwindling productive workforce : 줄어드는 생산 노동력
- local autonomous administrations : 지방 자치 행정부
- due to : ~때문에
- expanding elderly population : 팽창하는 노인 인구
- Organization for Economic Cooperation and Development = OECD
- infrastructure : 기반시설
- implementation : 시행
- of the opinion that : ~와 같은 의견이다
- all in all : 전체적으로 볼 때
- in terms of : ~의 관점에서
- social welfare : 사회 복지

영작체크

① 다른 선진국처럼, 국가는 이제 증가하는 기대수명과 감소하는 출생률 때문에 증가하는 숫자의 노인들의 심각한 사회 문제에 직면하고 있다.
(advanced countries / be faced with / life expectancy / decline / birth rate)

(모범영작) Like other advanced countries, the nation is now faced with a serious social problem of increasing numbers of old people because of the rising life expectancy and declining birth rate.

② 노인들의 개선되고 있는 복지와 건강과 관련하여, 중앙정부와 지방자치정부는 또한 그들을 위한 직업 기회를 확대하기 위한 노력에 집중할 필요가 있다.
(in connection with / welfare / local autonomous administration / job opportunity)

(모범영작) In connection with improving the welfare and health of aged people, the central government and local autonomous administrations also need to concentrate efforts to expand job opportunities for them.

③ 정부는 부부들이 더 많은 아이를 갖도록 격려하고 있기 때문에, 1960년 이래로 강제 시행되고 있는 출산 억제가 분명히 팽창하는 노인 인구 때문에, 줄어드는 생산노동력 관점에서 버려지고 있다. (encourage / birth control / discard / in view of / dwindle / workforce / elderly population)

(모범영작) As the government encourages couples to have more babies, birth control, which has been in force since 1960, is discarded apparently in view of the dwindling productive workforce due to the expanding elderly population.

07

1. The government's concessive draft for partial opening of the education sector is encountering mounting resistance not only from academic circles but also from civic groups.
2. They are also said to have been selling faculty seats, as well as doctor degrees.
3. It is common for students to enroll in language courses at foreign schools, mostly those in the United States, Canada, Australia and New Zealand, in a bid to enhance their English language ability and so they can find a job more easily after graduation.

주요표현

- concessive draft : 양보적 초안
- partial opening of the education sector : 교육부문의 부분적 개방
- academic circles : 학술분야
- civic groups : 시민단체
- Korean Teachers and Educational Workers Union : 전교조
- Word Trade Organization : 세계무역기구
- aims at : ~을 겨냥하다
- reportedly : 알려진 바에 의하면
- keep up with : ~을 유지하다
- controversial minister : 문제가 되는 장관
- a substantial number of : 상당한 숫자의
- tuition fee : 수업료
- doctor degrees : 박사학위
- In this regard : 이런 면에서
- enhance competitiveness : 경쟁력을 제고 하다

영작체크

① 교육부문의 부분적 개방에 대한 정부의 양보적 초안은 학술분야와 시민단체로부터 늘어나는 저항에 부딪치고 있다. (concessive draft / partial / education sector / not only ~ but also / academic circles / civic groups)

(모범영작) The government's concessive draft for partial opening of the education sector is encountering mounting resistance not only from academic circles but also from civic groups.

② 그들은 또한 박사학위 뿐만 아니라, 교수자리도 팔아 왔다고 한다.
(faculty seats / doctor degrees)

(모범영작) They are also said to have been selling faculty seats, as well as doctor degrees.

③ 학생들이 미국, 캐나다, 호주, 뉴질랜드에 있는 대부분의 것들인 외국학교에서, 그들의 영어능력을 높이려는 시도 속에서, 언어 수업에 등록하는 것은 흔한 일이다. 그래서 그들은 졸업 후에 보다 쉽게 직업을 찾을 수 있다. (enroll / in a bid to / enhance)

(모범영작) It is common for students to enroll in language courses at foreign schools, mostly those in the United States, Canada, Australia and New Zealand, in a bid to enhance their English language ability and so they can find a job more easily after graduation.

08

1. We are all dependent on water, no matter who we are, where we are and what we do, and we need it everyday.
2. Nevertheless, precious water is wasted and contaminated too often in too many places, with the quantity and quality of available water ever decreasing.
3. South Korea is already classified as a country short of water, but the people waste water like wealthy people spend money recklessly.
4. What's more serious is the ever-deteriorating quality of tap water, despite the government's repeated commitment to supply clean water.
5. Needless to say, saving water makes an effective key to conserve water resources.

주요표현

- United Nations-designated special day : 유엔이 지정한 특별한 날
- no matter who : 누가 ~ 한다 해도
- contaminate : 오염시키다
- recklessly : 무모하게도
- what's more serious : 더욱 심각한 것은
- ground water : 지하수
- irrigation : 관개시설
- needless to say : 말할 필요 없이

영작체크

① 우리는 모두 우리가 누구이건, 우리가 어디에 있건, 우리가 무엇을 하건, 물에 의존하고 있고, 우리는 매일 그것을 필요로 한다. (be dependent on / no matter who)

(모범영작) We are all dependent on water, no matter who we are, where we are and what we do, and we need it everyday.

② 그럼에도 불구하고, 귀중한 물은 아주 많은 지역에서 아주 종종 낭비되고 오염되고 있으며, 이용 가능한 많은 양과 질의 물이 계속 감소되고 있다.
(Nevertheless / contaminate / available)

(모범영작) Nevertheless, precious water is wasted and contaminated too often in too many places, with the quantity and quality of available water ever decreasing.

③ 남한은 이미 물 부족 국가로 분류되고 있지만, 사람들은 마치 부자들이 돈을 무모하게 쓰듯이 낭비하고 있다. (be classified as / short of / recklessly)

(모범영작) South Korea is already classified as a country short of water, but the people waste water like wealthy people spend money recklessly.

④ 더욱 심각한 것은, 깨끗한 물을 공급하려는 정부의 반복된 노력에도 불구하고 수돗물의 계속 나빠지는 질이다. (ever-deteriorating / tap water / despite / commitment)

(모범영작) What's more serious is the ever-deteriorating quality of tap water, despite the government's repeated commitment to supply clean water.

⑤ 말할 것도 없이, 물을 절약하는 것이 수자원을 아끼는 효과적인 열쇠이다.
(Needless to say / conserve / water resources)

(모범영작) Needless to say, saving water makes an effective key to conserve water resources.

09

1. Obscene spam mail being sent to Internet and mobile phone users randomly has emerged as a serious social evil that must be eradicated as soon as possible for the health of society and particularly for the youth.
2. No communication means is regarded as more convenient and efficient than e-mails.
3. What makes the matter worse is the infiltration of obscene spam into the Web sites or cell phones of middle and high school students and even elementary school kids.

주요표현

- obscene spam mail : 음란 스팸 메일
- lewd e-mails : 음탕한 이메일
- reinforce : 강화하다
- subscribers : 가입자

영작체크

① 인터넷과 이동전화 사용자에게 무작위로 보내지고 있는 음란 스팸 메일이 사회, 특히 젊은이들을 위해 가능한 빨리 제거되어야 하는 심각한 사회악으로서 나타나고 있다.
(Obscene / spam mail / mobile phone / randomly / social evil / eradicate)

(모범영작) Obscene spam mail being sent to Internet and mobile phone users randomly has emerged as a serious social evil that must be eradicated as soon as possible for the health of society and particularly for the youth.

② 어떤 커뮤니케이션 수단도 이메일보다 편리하거나 효과적으로 간주되는 수단은 없다.
(be regarded as / more ~ than)

(모범영작) No communication means is regarded as more convenient and efficient than e-mails.

③ 문제를 더욱 악화시키는 것은, 웹사이트나 중, 고등학생과 심지어 초등학교 아동들의 휴대전화까지 음란 스팸이 침투하고 있는 것이다.
(makes the matter worse / infiltration)

(모범영작) What makes the matter worse is the infiltration of obscene spam into the

Web sites or cell phones of middle and high school students and even elementary school kids.

10

1. Some provincial universities will get a lot of benefits as part of the government plan to develop them as regional research and development centers.
2. To ensure active participation of parents in the decision-making process of school policies, the ministry will institutionalize a tripartite committee for residents, parents and teachers.
3. To ensure open and transparent educational policies, 20 percent of responsible positions in the education ministry will be filled through public subscriptions, while a special section will be set up on the ministry's official Web site for two-way communication channel between educational policy makers and the public.

주요표현

- mergers and acquisitions : 합병과 인수
- meeting assessment criteria : 평가 기준을 충족시키는
- reduce soaring private educational costs : 치솟는 사교육비를 줄이다
- Education and Human Resources Development Minister : 교육 인적자원 개발부 장관
- provincial universities : 지방대학
- trigger fierce backlash : 거센 반대를 만들다
- government-sponsored organizations : 정부가 후원하는 기관들
- institutionalize : 제도화하다
- tripartite committee : 3자 위원회
- collapse of public education : 공교육의 붕괴
- transparent educational policies : 투명한 교육 정책
- public subscriptions : 공개 가입
- two-way communication channel : 쌍방 커뮤니케이션 채널

영작체크

① 일부 지방대학들은 지역 연구 개발 중심지로서 그것들을 개발하려는 정부의 계획의 일부로서, 많은 혜택을 얻을 것이다. (provincial universities / benefits / regional)

....

....

(모범영작) Some provincial universities will get a lot of benefits as part of the government plan to develop them as research and development centers.

② 학교정책의 의사결정 과정에서 부모들의 적극적 참여를 보증하기 위해, 장관은 주민, 부모, 교사의 3자 위원회를 제도화할 것이다.
(ensure / institutionalize / tripartite committee)

_____

_____

(모범영작) To ensure active participation of parents in the decision-making process of school policies, the ministry will institutionalize a tripartite committee for residents, parents and teachers.

③ 개방되고 투명한 교육정책을 보증하기 위해, 교육부에 20퍼센트의 책임 있는 자리가 공개 가입을 통해 채워질 것이며, 반면에 특별부문이 교육정책 입안자와 국민 사이에 쌍방 커뮤니케이션 채널을 위해 장관의 공식 웹페이지에 만들어 질 것이다.
(transparent / subscription / be set up)

_____

_____

(모범영작) To ensure open and transparent educational policies, 20 percent of responsible positions in the education ministry will be filled through public subscriptions, while a special section will be set up on the ministry's official Web site for two-way communication channel between educational policy makers and the public.

11

1. Young Korean parents are spoiling their kids with excessive protection.
2. It is very likely that you may be attacked in similar situations when not supported by others nearby.
3. It is very natural for parents to protect and love their children, but we should also realize that parents' love is very exclusive and the object of that love is confined to our own children only.
4. When I was in my thirties, I traveled all over the world to sell Korean manufactured goods.
5. Whether I was in New York, London or even Africa, rarely did I see a kid running around and disturbing others.

6. Their young parents always watched them to make sure they were doing what they were told to do.
7. In the same vein, our children must be taught discipline to refrain themselves.
8. Some young parents may insist that troubles rise from generation gaps we now experience in Korean society, but this is not a matter of generation gaps.
9. I must insist that our schoolteachers should be authorized to punish bad students as in the past.

주요표현

- spoil : 망가뜨리다
- confined to : ~에 국한되다
- rarely did I see : (도치구문) 나는 거의 ~도 보지 못했다.
- to make sure : ~을 분명히 하기 위해
- in the same vein : ~같은 맥락에서
- generation gap : 세대차
- exclusive : 배타적인 / 독점적인
- when I was in my thirties : 내가 30세대에
- are left unchecked : 버릇없이 남아있다
- refrain themselves : 삼가하다
- authorize : 인가하다

영작체크

① 젊은 한국 부모들은 지나친 보호로 그들의 아이들을 망가뜨리고 있다. (spoil / excessive)

(모범영작) Young Korean parents are spoiling their kids with excessive protection.

② 여러분은 가까이 있는 다른 사람들에 의해 지지 받지 못할 때, 유사한 상황에서 공격 당할 수 있는 가능성이 매우 많다. (it is very likely that / attack / support)

(모범영작) It is very likely that you may be attacked in similar situations when not supported by others nearby.

③ 부모들이 그들의 자녀들을 보호하고 사랑하는 것은 매우 자연스런 것이지만, 우리는 또한 부모들의 사랑이 매우 배타적이고, 그런 사랑의 목표는 우리 자신의 자녀에게만 국한된다는 것을 깨달아야 한다. (exclusive / object / be confined to)

(모범영작) It is very natural for parents to protect and love their children, but we should also realize that parents' love is very exclusive and the object of that love is confined to our own children only.

④ 내가 30세대였을 때, 나는 한국의 제조제품을 팔기 위해 세계 여행을 했었다.
(in one's / manufactured goods)

(모범영작) When I was in my thirties, I traveled all over the world to sell Korean manufactured goods.

⑤ 내가 뉴욕이나 런던, 심지어 아프리카에 있었던 간에, 나는 어떤 아이가 뛰어다니면서 다른 사람을 방해하는 것을 본 적이 거의 거의 없다. (whether / rarely / disturb)

(모범영작) Whether I was in New York, London or even Africa, rarely did I see a kid running around and disturbing others.

⑥ 그들의 부모들을 항상 그들이 분명히 그들에게 행동하라고 이야기 들었던 것을 하라고 지켜보았다. (make sure / on the contrary)

(모범영작) Their young parents always watched them to make sure they were doing what they were told to do.

⑦ 같은 맥락에서, 우리의 아이들에게는 스스로를 삼가도록 규율을 가르쳐야 한다.
(in the same vein / discipline / refrain)

(모범영작) In the same vein, our children must be taught discipline to refrain themselves.

⑧ 일부 젊은 부모들은 아마도 문제들이 우리가 지금 한국 사회에서 경험하고 있는 세대 차로부터 생긴다고 주장할지도 모른다. (insist / generation gap)

(모범영작) Some young parents may insist that troubles rise from generation gaps we now experience in Korean society, but this is not a matter of generation gaps.

⑨ 나는 우리의 교사들에게 과거에서처럼 나쁜 학생들을 벌주는 것이 허락되어야 한다고 주장해야 한다. (authorize / punish)

(모범영작) I must insist that our schoolteachers should be authorized to punish bad students as in the past.

3 종합 영작문 연습

01 한반도의 긴장을 고조시키고 있는 북한의 핵 위협의 측면에서, 이곳에 주둔하고 있는 37,000 미군의 역할과 중요성이 지금처럼 많이 인식된 적도 없다.

- in light of : ~에 비추어 볼 때
- tension : 긴장
- heighten : 고조시키다
- peninsula : (한) 반도
- troops : 주둔하다

02 국민들의 관심은 이들 군대들의 재배치에 대해 서울과 워싱턴 사이의 협상에 초점이 맞추어져 있다.

- be focused on : ~에 초점을 맞추다
- negotiation : 협상
- realignment : 재배치

03 일반적으로 워싱턴은 평양과의 핵 교착상태 처리 협상의 해결이 있기 전에 재배치를 추진해야 할 것으로 믿고 있다고 한다.

- it is generally believed that = they generally believe that : 라고 일반적으로 믿어지다
- push ahead with : 추진하다
- nuclear standoff : 핵 교착상태

04 정부는 또한 한반도에서 평화유지뿐만 아니라 국가 안전을 손상되지 않도록 하기 위해, 재배치를 대처하기 위한 적절한 조치를 취할 필요가 있다.

- take appropriate steps : 적절한 조치를 취하다
- re-deployment : 재배치
- cope with : ~에 대처하다
- keep ~ intact : 그대로 놔두다

05 50세와 60세대의 사람들이 사회적 박탈감을 느끼고 있는 것은 당연하다.

- in their 50s and 60s : ~ 나이가 50대와 60대
- a sense of social deprivation : 사회적 박탈감
- It is natural that : ~은 당연하다

06 중요한 것은, 그들이 몇 살이냐에 상관없이, 얼마나 적극적이고 현명하게 사람들이 인생에 종사하느냐 하는 것이다.

- be engaged in : ~에 종사하다
- regardless of : ~에 관계없이

07 현재 40대와 50대의 사람들은, 단지 그들이 늙었다는 이유로, 조만간 직장에서 불필요하게 되어질 것이라는 것을 두려워하고 있다.

- currently: 현재
- be made redundant : 불필요하게 되다
- sooner or later : 조만간

08

전자는 후자보다 세계 시장에서 첨단기술과 경쟁하기 위해서 훨씬 더 가치가 있다.

- the former: 전자
- far more : 훨씬 더
- cutting-edge technology : 첨단기술
- the latter: 후자
- compete with : 경쟁하다
- global market : 세계 시장

09

그들은 한국어를 영어로 그리고 반대의 경우로도 번역할 수 있는 한 한국인을 고용하고 있었다.

- translate ~ into : 번역하다
- vice versa : 반대의 경우도 마찬가지

10

정신적, 육체적 피로는 몸과 마음의 성장을 지체시키고, 그것은 종종 정신질환을 야기시키기도 한다.

- mental and physical exhaustion : 정신적 육체적 피로
- retard : 지체시키다
- psychosomatic illness : 정신질환

11

학업 성적과 지적인 능력이 개성의 유일한 척도로서 사용되어서는 안 된다.

- academic points : 학업 성적
- appraisal : (평가) 척도
- intellectual faculties : 지적인 능력

12

점점 많은 숫자의 사람들이 그들의 신용카드빚을 갚지 못해 불량거래자 명단에 오르고 있다.

- a growing number of : 점점 많은 숫자의
- blacklist : 불량거래자 명단에 오르다
- credit card debts : 신용카드빚

13

이런 면에서, 북한은 높아 가는 긴장 문제들을 제거하기 위해 미국과의 핵 교착상태를 평화롭게 해결해야만 한다.

- in this regard : 이런 면에서
- nuclear standoff : 핵 교착상태
- mounting tension : 높아가는 긴장
- resolve : 해결하다
- removec : 제거하다

14

부모들은 아이들의 개인적 특성과 능력을 고려하지 않으면서, 그들의 이상에 맞춰 자녀를 기를 수 있다는 잘못된 생각을 포기해야 한다.

- give up : 포기하다
- raise : 기르다
- characteristics : 특성
- false belief : 잘못된 생각
- take into account : 고려하다
- capabilities : 능력

모범답안

1. In light of North Korea's nuclear threat heightening tensions on the peninsula, the role and importance of 37,000 American troops stationed here has never been recognized as much as it is now.
2. The public's attention is focused on negotiations between Seoul and Washington over the realignment of these troops.
3. It is generally believed that Washington will push ahead with the relocation even before the settlement of the nuclear standoff with Pyongyang.
4. The government also needs to take appropriate steps to cope with the redeployment in order to keep national security intact as well as maintain peace on the peninsula.
5. It is natural that people in their 50s and 60s are feeling a sense of social deprivation.
6. What is important is how actively and wisely people are engaged in life, regardless of how old they are.
7. Currently, people in their 40s and 50s are afraid they will be made redundant at work sooner or later only because they are old.
8. The former is far more valuable than the latter so as to compete with cutting-edge technology in the global market.
9. They were employing one Korean that could translate Korean into English and vice versa.
10. Mental and physical exhaustion retards the growth of body and mind, and it often causes a psychosomatic illness.
11. One's academic points and intellectual faculties should not be used as the sole appraisal for standard of personality.
12. A growing number of young people are being blacklisted for failing to pay their credit card debts.
13. In this regard, North Korea ought to peacefully resolve its nuclear standoff with the United State to remove mounting tensions.
14. Parents should give up their false belief that they can raise their children to their ideals, without taking into account of the children's personal characteristics and capabilities.

에세이 영작문

신경향 종합영작문 클리닉 PART IV.

1 훌륭한 영작문 10계명

좋은 영작문은 탄탄한 문법 구문 지식과 작문 규칙에 토대를 두며, 다음 10가지 원칙이 작문을 돋보이며 만들어준다.

1. 우아한 문체보다는 단순한 묘사가 더 좋다.

2. 이국적 표현보다는 친숙한 단어를 써라.

3. 낭만적 문체보다는 보통 문체가 더 좋다: 간결하게 써라.

4. 형용사나 부사보다는 명사나 동사가 더 좋다: 분명한 진술문을 사용하라.

5. 그림동사(picture nouns)와 동작동사(actions verbs)를 사용하라: 묘사적 문장을 만들어라.

6. 짧은 단어가 있을 때는 긴 단어를 쓰지 마라.

7. 단순한 비유를 정복하라. 묘사는 흥미로워야 한다.

8. 복잡한 문장(complicated sentence)보다는 단순한 문장(simple sentence)이 더 좋다.

9. 문장의 길이를 다양하게 써라.

10. 능동태를 써라: 능동형이 이야기를 활력있게 한다.

2 영작문의 단계

1. 영작문의 과정

(1) 주제에 대한 단어들을 열거하거나 브레인스토밍 한다. (pre-writing : listing)
    ex. Make a list of words about music.

(2) 주어진 단어들을 사용하여 문장을 써본다. (Writing the first draft)
    ex. Using words from your list, write a sentence about music.

(3) 쓴 문장이 올바르게 쓰였는지 확인하고 다시 쓴다.
(Revising: Ask yourself if your sentence makes sense)
    ex. Rewrite your sentence, using one or more of these improvements:
        (a) Add an important detail, (b) change boring words to interesting words, or (c) move some words around.

(4) 편집하고 철자나 대문자, 구두점 등을 점검한다. (Editing and Proofreading)
    ex. Check your revised sentences for errors in spelling, capitalization, or punctuation.

(5) 수정된 글을 옮겨 쓰며 글을 완성한다. (Publishing)
    ex. Copy your revised and edited sentence in your best handwriting.

2. 에세이 영작문 7단계 공식

(1) 사상을 생각나는 대로 열거하라.
(2) 주제를 한정시켜라.
(3) Thesis Statement를 쓴다.
(4) 본문(body)을 계획한다.
(5) 결론(conclusion)을 계획한다.
(6) 글을 쓴다.
(7) 수정하고 다듬는다.

3 에세이 단락의 구성

1. 전체 단락(PARAGRAPH)의 구성

에세이 영작문은 서론·본론·결론의 3요소를 유지한다.

서론 INTRODUCTION

- **일반서술부**(General Statements) : 에세이를 읽을 사람의 관심을 유도한다.

  ① 에세이 제목을 자신의 글에 끌어들인다.
  ② 주제와 관련된 흥미로운 이야기나 정보를 이용한다.

- **논제서술부**(Thesis Statements) : 에세이의 주제 혹은 전체적인 구성을 언급한다. 대개 서론 끝에 위치하며 에세이에서 가장 중요한 문장이다. Thesis Statement는 글의 main idea를 제공한다.

  ① 에세이의 주제와 요지를 간결하게 정리한다.
  ② 글의 전체적인 구성과 주제의 내용을 언급한다.

본론 BODY

본론은 Thesis Statement를 분명하고 자세히 설명해 주며, 주제문(topic sentence)을 포함하여 몇 개의 부연 문장으로 구성된다. 부연 문장(supporting sentence)은 이유, 예시, 사실 및 통계를 이용하여 주제문을 전개하여 설명해 가는 부분이다. 이때 구체적이고 사실적인 의견을 제시하여야 한다.

결론 CONCLUSION

주제를 요약(summary)하는 단락으로 다른 표현으로 서론 부분을 재진술(restatement)하거나 주제에 대한 자신의 최종 의견을 쓴다. 결론은 단락들의 내용을 종합하여 정리하며 의미 없는 어구를 나열하지 않도록 한다.

① 재진술(restatement) : Thesis statement를 단어와 문장구조를 paraphrase하여 부연 설명하고, 본론의 핵심이 되는 부분을 다시 요약한다.
② 최종의견(final comment) : 주제에 대한 자신의 의견과 문제에 대한 해결책을 제안한다. 그리고 생각의 여지를 남기는 질문으로 끝을 맺으면 좀더 세련된 느낌을 준다.

2. 주제문(TOPIC SENTENCE)

모든 다른 문장이 설명해 주는 것으로, 대개 글의 요약이나 제목을 의미한다. 통일성(unity)과 일관성(coherence)을 유지하여 정확하게 쓰는 것이 중요하다. 주제문에서 문제를 제기하거나 자신의 생각과 견해를 밝힌다. 이때 일반적인 사실을 기술한 다음에 구체적인 내용을 쓰는 것이 중요하다. 주제문은 단락의 첫머리나 중간 혹은 마지막에 올 수 있는데, 대개는 첫째나 둘째 문장이 주제문인 경우가 많다.

3. 본문의 전개

주제문의 내용을 부연, 설명해 간다. 묘사(description), 예증(example), 설득(persuasion), 비교/대조(comparison/contrast), 유추(analogy), 분류(classification) 등의 기법으로 본문을 전개한다.

(1) 분류에 쓰이는 표현들
- be classified (구분되다)
- be categorized (유형짓다)
- group A into B (A를 B로 구분짓다)
- be divided into (~으로 나누다)

(2) 비교(comparison)에 많이 쓰이는 표현
- alike / like (~와 같은)
- identical (같은)
- equivalent (동등한)
- similar / similarities (유사한 / 유사성)
- also (또한)
- resembles (~을 닮다)
- just as (~와 똑같이)
- likewise (마찬가지로)
- corresponds to (~와 일치하여)
- comparable to (~에 비유되는)
- by the same token (~와 같이)

(3) 대조(contrast)에 많이 쓰이는 표현
- unlike (~와 달리)
- different / differences (다른 / 차이점)
- in contrast (대조적으로)
- worse / better (~보다 더 나쁜 / 더 좋은)
- whereas (~인 반면에)
- conversely (대조적으로)
- but (그러나)
- on the other hand (한편)
- more than / less than / fewer than (~보다 많은 / 적은)

4 토플 에세이(TWE)

1. TWE (Test of Written English)

토플 에세이는 제한 시간 30분 동안 주어진 주제에 대해 논리적으로 생각을 전개하고, 자신의 논리를 충분히 뒷받침할 근거와 세부 사항을 250자에서 350자 정도 기술한다.

2. 작문 등급

에세이 점수는 0점에서 6점까지 분포되며, 주제 관련성, 단락구성, 문장구성력, 어휘구사력, 그리고 문법성에 따라 성적이 좌우된다.

3. 토플 에세이 유형

ETS(Educational Testing Service)에서 새로 나온 에세이 주제는 185개이며, 4가지 유형으로 분류된다.

(1) Detail : 원인, 결과, 이유 등을 설명하는 문제

> *ex.* 0015 Neighbors are the people who live near us. In your opinion, what are the qualities of a good neighbor? Use specific details and examples in your answer.

(2) Preference : 둘 중에 하나를 선택해서 자신의 주장을 피력하는 문제

> *ex.* 0047 Some people prefer to work for a large company. Others prefer to work for a small company. Which would you prefer? Use specific reasons and details to support your choice.

(3) Agree / Disagree : 주어진 진술에 대한 찬반을 묻는 문제

ex. 0011 Do you agree or disagree with the following statement? Universities should give the same amount of money to their students' sports activities as they give to their university libraries. Use specific reasons and examples to support your opinion.

(4) Compare / Contrast : 비교 / 대조하는 문제

ex. 0005 A company has announced that it wishes to build a large factory near your community. Discuss the advantages and disadvantages of this new influence on your community. Do you support or oppose the factory? Explain your position.

토플 Essay의 예와 배점

Sample Topic A:
Do you agree or disagree with the following statement:
Teachers should make learning enjoyable and fun for their students.
Use specific reasons and examples to support your opinion.

ESSAY (6점)

I do strongly support the idea that teachers should make learning enjoyable and fun for the students. This I support with the following reasons.
First let us take the psychological component of a student. A child or student will be more receptive, to anything including studies, if the subject matter is presented in an interesting and enjoyable manner. If not there is every likelihood that the student will be unwilling or will reject the matter presented as he considers studying is a burden on him.

My second point is that the present day student faces tremendous amount of distraction such as interesting television programmes, drugs, distractions from opposite sexes and many more. To get the student away from all these and to get him interested in studies there is obviously no other way than to make learning interesting.

The present day students are also pressured with tremendous amount of competition from other students. With this mounting pressure on them coupled with the hugh expectation of the parents, it will lighten the burden on the young students with a more acceptable form of presentation that is in an enjoyable and fun manner.

Retention is another factor that should considered important. Any presentation which is given an interesting or enjoyable manner can be retained well by the students. If the subject matter presented is uninteresting then there is strong likelihood the student will forget the subject matter presented in days or even hours.

When presenting a subject the teacher should create a desire amongst the student to crave for knowledge on the subject and this can certainly be obtained if the subject matter is presented in a fun and enjoyable manner.

It can also be said that the present day communication system is so advanced and these are ample teaching aids and techniques to make teaching fun and enjoyable. So why not utilise the opportunities to the full so that the student at the receiving end can benefit to the full.

Last but not least I wish to say that by making teaching fun and enjoyable the life expectancy of both the students and the teachers can be extended.

배점기준(6점)
1. 구성력과 전개의 조화
2. 주제를 효과적으로 쓴다.
3. 적절하게 세부 사항을 사용하여 전개한다.
4. 언어의 일관성을 유지한다.
5. 구문적 다양함과 적절한 어휘 선택을 한다.

ESSAY (5점)

"Teachers should make learning enjoyable and fun for their students". I do completely agree with this statements. I believe that there have been many studies done on this subject, and they all indicate that if children during their first years of schooling associate learning as enjoyable and fun they will learn the subjects and retain more than if presented on a dull way. The trend in learning and education appears to support this idea.

The role of the teacher now days is more than just giving away a number of facts for students to learn. By making learning fun and enjoyable the student will also get motivated and probably do some research or outside class investigation to enrich his or her own knowledge. Some may say that this is a lot of work for the teachers. However if you look at all the technology available, for example computer educational programs, educational videos etc.; they all try make the learning process enjoyable and fun. It is easier for teachers to plan their classes by using such materials. Students benefits as well since they are learning without associating the process as been a tedious chore needed to get a grade and pass a class.

I do believe that in the long run both students and teachers will achieve great results and a sense of a well accomplished job by approaching learning as an enjoyable and fun activity.

배점기준(5점)
1. 일반적으로 잘 구성되고 전개된다.
2. 세부 사실을 이용하여 예증하고 있다.
3. 어느 정도의 구문적 다양함과 다양한 어휘를 구사한다.

ESSAY (4점)

In my point of view. I do agree that teacher should make leaning enjoyable and fun for their students for the following reasons.

Firstly, students may pay more attention of what the teacher says. Instead of talking to somebody else. they may concentrate on their work. Since the most important thing is that they are not bored by the lesson.

Secondly, the teacher will be more welcomed by students For one may compare a friendly, funny teacher to those boring, strict one.
Thirdly, the lively environment of learning makes students Rave a high spirit of learning. Students may actively participate in class activities. Thus, through different approaches of teaching, students may learn more or be more enjoyable.

All in all, the imperative purpose is to make students feel learning in a relaxed way not stressing too much pressure on them. Gradually, they will find interest in learning. Therefore, I strongly agree that teachers should make learning enjoyable and fun for their students.

배점기준(4점)
1. 주제는 적절하지만 부분적으로 다루고 있다.
2. 적절하게 구성되고 전개된다.
3. 일부 세부 사항을 써서 부연설명 한다.
4. 적절하지만 일관되지 않은 구문과 어휘를 쓴다.
5. 의미가 통하지 않는 오류를 범하고 있다.

ESSAY (3점)

Teachers should make leaning enjoyable and fun for their students. Do you agree or disagree with the statement? Give reasons to support your opinion.

If my teachers make leaning enjoyable and fun for my class. I agree that. because I think it is a good way to make students remember in subject and want to study in school so I am a student in school and university long time I think I know the felling of students when teachers teach. Some teachers are strong in subject. They stay on time and teach all of time until finch. We didn't have break times or time for relax. After class we are very tired and we couldn't to remember that the teacher teach us. We know nothing, but some teacher knows about that he tries to teach us and have time to relax or enjoyable for example we take together in class or have some game to play together about subject that the teacher teaches us or have break time for drink water. I like this way to study. I think it makes us understand and want to study more than another way. I think I can say intersent every students I like if teachers should make leaning enjoyable and fun for their students. I agree.

배점기준(3점)
1. 부적절한 구성과 전개를 한다.
2. 부적절하고 불충분한 세부 사항을 써 내용 부연에 부족함이 있다.
3. 어휘 선택이 눈에 띄게 부적절하다.
4. 문장 구조나 용법에서 오류가 많다.

ESSAY(2점)

The teacher is important for school, most students don't like them. Sometimes we can finds to that teacher was boring. I think of teacher should make learning enjoyable and fun for their students. because they could by means of learning and fun get many students, another they could be better teacher and good skill from education.

And then if teacher should make learning **ciriouses** with their students, I think this way not good for teacher: For example the student will be fear and dislike to the teacher. Beside they don't like enjoy their class. maybe they cut it.

Good as well as saying the teacher is basic of education in the contrary. In the **concult** I like teacher learning enjoyable and funny and then I'll be interested with class and get many things. That is better for me.

배점기준(2점)
1. 구성과 전개가 문제가 많다.
2. 세부 항목이 부적절하거나 불충분하다.
3. 문장 구조나 용법이 심각하게 오류가 많다.
4. 요점이 맞지 않는다.

ESSAY(1점)

Teachers should make learning enjoyable and fun for their students. I think teachers should make learning enjoyable and fun for their student. Do you agree or disagree with the statement? Yes, I do. Why do I think so? Because the teacher is teaching the students. And the student is teaching the teachers. Of course me too. This is very **impotant**. It is don't forget us!

배점기준(1점)
1. 일관성이 없다.
2. 전개에 문제가 많다.
3. 심각하고 계속적인 작문 오류가 있다.

Sample Topic B:
Supporters of technology say that it solves problems and makes life better. Opponents argue that technology creates new problems that may threaten or damage the quality of life. Using one or two examples, discuss these two positions. Which view of technology do you support? Why?

View Sample Essay with Score of : 6, 5, 4, 3, 2, 1

ESSAY (6점)

These are several viewpoints on the implications of technological change and advancement and such schools of thought which considerably vary have their respective validity. Technological change has its advantages and disadvantages. For one, it is true that it partly solves problems and makes life better. At the same time, technological changes may likely create new problems thereby threatening or damaging quality of life. In the developing economies, for instance, technological advantages has both its merits and demerits. The introduction and seeming acceptability and usefulness of computers have somehow helped increase the efficiency of several firms. It is not only in the industrial sector that technological change proven to be very effective. In the agricultural sector, for example, the introduction of new technologies in increasing production has been very effective in expanding agricultural produce. These are just a few examples to illustrate the advantages of technological advancement.

On the other hand, countries should be more careful on their choice of technology since it must be noted that while certain types of technology are adaptable to developed economies the same type of technology may not fit the environment of developing countries due to differing economic, social, cultural, and political factors. For example, infrastructure improvements such as a construction of irrigation dam in the mountains of the Philippines where several natives reside may likely be resisted by the population due to cultural factors. They may prefer not to have such improvements in view of traditional values. Another example is the pollution impact of some technological improvements particularly in the industrial sectors.

The choice and adaptability of new technology should therefore be carefully studied. The short, medium, and long term impact of such technology is very important particulary for developing economies. The benefits should always be greater than the costs.
I am inclined to support both positions because both views have their own validity. However, I am more convinced that technological advancement is heilly beneficial to countries so long as they are aware of the disadvantages of such technology.

ESSAY(5점)

Technology by definition refers to the improvement of the technical know how and advancement of machinery to improve the working systems in the human society. In a away this looks a very good idea in that mans' work would be made much faster and less laborious. Machines which are the main implements of technology have a major advantage to mans' ways of life. Take for example an aeroplane, which being a product of advance in **tecnology** has made all corners of the earth look like they are only **centimetres** apart. It has made the means of communication which prior to its development was very difficult much easier and less risky. Travelling to many parts of the world which are very many miles apart now only takes a few hours or days where as this used to take days or even months.

On the other hand technology has created a number of new **harzards** to the health of societies. The machines make life easy but also expose people to new problems. In the example considered above transportation has become easier by planes but these planes also expose people to accidents which have become so numerous and clam many lives daily. As we all know that a majority of these machines use fuel and that to use the fuel it has to burn there are new products which we introduced into our **enviroment**. These new products include gases from automobiles which pollute the air we breathe. These gases expose us to lung diseases, cancers and number of new ailments which have not yet been fully explored.

In conclusion I think that although advances in technology may seem favorable there are a lot of harzards which it introduces into our ways of life.

ESSAY (4점)

I agree with the opponents of technology say that technology creates new problems that may threaten or damage the quality of life. The most serious problem is the pollution. Toxic wastes are being dumped into rivers, lakes and even out atmosphere. Fish and other marine live cannot survive in polluted rivers and oceans. Also, toxic gases are being produced by cars, factories and planes. This is the main source which causes the acid rain. Acid rain has done a great damage to the forest that the quanlity of trees are reducing day by day. The ozone layer—a protective layer that surrounding us in the atmosphere is **carring** away by wasted chemicals. That means we are lossing our protective layer and letting **ultroviolet** to pass through. And for us, we are breathing in a lot of polluted air which may make us ill or sometimes may cause death.

Technology may solve a lot of problems but the point is the result of technology gives us **disavantages** more than **avantages**. So I a on the side of the opponents.

ESSAY (3점)

In my own points of view I support technology can solve problems and makes life better. Such as development of computer. Computer helps human solves thousand of problems especially science. A lot of calculation was so complex. It is impossible count them from normal method It should use a very fast computer in order to compute it. Super conductor, one of the hot technology topic. A lot of scientists study this kind of stuff. It is a very important stuff. If we can use it in normal way. That is wonderful. We can easily solve the big problem, "energy". Because super conductor has a special mental. It can pass through the energy without losing. It is a Hi-technology's symbol.

But technology also created a lot of problem. Such as industry unless thing. Human feel dizzy from then. A lot of vehicles running on the road. Creating much CO_2. Affect the earth's nature condition Recently. The weather was so bad. Because of the CO_2. CO_2 blocks the sun light. So the weather was inconsiderable.

Finally, I support technology. Because it is more benefit.

ESSAY (2점)

The main point is technology, and what does technology, and what does technology do in our life, before anything we should suggest to some **technolgy's** working way in daily life.
Technology would be very useful but, in some condition for example as a nature distributing which it would be very dangerous, but it could be very important in other way for better live and make the life's things to do easier.

Supporting technology is very important–and it would make the useful way of using technology, because it needs the supporters and investing to find more and more progress in the technology.

But sometimes technology makes some problem that I mention in the beginning of essay and it would very dangerous in some ways. For example factories trash makes some problems and makes the water dirty and it's damage wouldn't be not quality easy.

At the end I would like to say that: supporting of technology will be helpful and make life easier, but technology must be very careful to not be a danger and risky.

ESSAY(1점)

Now a days, in the life the technology it solves problems. But damage the quality of the life is very important. Because the many people to the quality of life is very high than the yesterday **socizat**. They are use or buys goods is more good then yesterday. So the many people to need the high quality are too many.

토플 Essay 연습-토론 및 첨삭 지도

▶▶▶ **유형 1.** 원인 / 결과 / 이유 설명하기

1 People attend college or university for many different reasons (for example, new experiences, career preparation, increased knowledge). Why do you think people attend college or university? Use specific reasons and examples to support your answer.

2

Nowadays, food has become easier to prepare. Has this change improved the way people live? Use specific reasons and examples to support your answer.

3

If you could change one important thing about your hometown, what would you change? Use reasons and specific examples to support your answer.

유형 2. 2개의 견해 중 선택하여 설명하기

1

It has been said, "Not everything that is learned is contained in books." Compare and contrast knowledge gained from experience with knowledge gained from books. In your opinion, which source is more important? Why?

2

It has recently been announced that a large shopping center may be built in your neighborhood. Do you support or oppose this plan? Why? Use specific reasons and details to support your answer.

3

It has recently been announced that a new movie theater may be built in your neighborhood. Do you support or oppose this plan? Why? Use specific reasons and details to support your answer.

▶▶▶ **유형 3.** 찬성과 반대 설명하기

1

Do you agree or disagree with the following statement? Parents are the best teachers. Use specific reasons and examples to support your answer.

2

Do you agree or disagree with the following statement? Universities should give the same amount of money to their students' sports activities as they give to their university libraries. Use specific reasons and examples to support your opinion.

3 Do you agree or disagree with the following statement? Television, newspapers, magazines, and other media pay too much attention to the personal lives of famous people such as public figures and celebrities. Use specific reasons and details to explain your opinion.

유형 4. 비교와 대조하기

1

Some people believe that the best way of learning about life is by listening to the advice of family and friends. Other people believe that the best way of learning about life is through personal experience. Compare the advantages of these two different ways of learning about life. Which do you think is preferable? Use specific examples to support your preference.

2

Some people think that children should begin their formal education at a very early age and should spend most of their time on school studies. Others believe that young children should spend most of their time playing. Compare these two views. Which view do you agree with? Why?

3

The government has announced that it plans to build a new university. Some people think that your community would be a good place to locate the university. Compare the advantages and disadvantages of establishing a new university in your community. Use specific details in your discussion.